Picturemaking

Butterick Publishing

Edited by Yvonne Deutch

Library of Congress Catalog Number 77-020471

ISBN: 0-88421-057-X

Published in the United States of America by
Butterick Publishing
161 Sixth Avenue
New York, · NY 10013
A Division of American Can Company

© Marshall Cavendish Limited

Printed in Great Britain

Introduction

Would you like to make beautiful pictures – your own originals which you'll be proud to display? *Picturemaking* will show you how to achieve unique results – and you don't have to be a trained artist or possess any special skills. You simply take the whole idea of making pictures out of the traditional easel and board approach, and into the realm of new and imaginative design techniques.

Picturemaking provides an excellent grounding in the basic areas of color, perspective and proportion by using an amazingly wide variety of projects and many different materials. Learn as you go with easy-to-follow text, clear diagrams and gorgeous illustrations. You may feel that you want to start with a bright, modern canvas, in which case the chapter on instant abstract painting will appeal to the budding Picasso; for a charming, rather nostalgic mood, make some silhouette pictures and build up a family group. The needlewoman of the family is included too, with the inclusion of several delightful stitchery pictures.

The range of projects will appeal to everyone – you can learn how to hand-tint prints, how to do spatter painting, how to make wonderful scenic murals, collages and mosaics – and there are plenty of pin and thread designs for the enthusiasts in this field. As a final touch we show you how to mount your work, and how to make a variety of frames to complement your pictures. *Picture making* will not only provide you with lots of patterns and guidelines, but will also inspire your own inventiveness and creativity.

Contents

Reproductions past and present

A wonderful treasury of pictures has been bequeathed to us over the centuries. If you are unable to travel to museums and art galleries to view the originals, many great pictures are available in reproduction form—in prints, in illustrated books, and of course in postcards. Many people love to have a good reproduction in their home, but nowadays the cost of good prints is staggering. In the following projects some fascinating techniques are shown which enable the most inexperienced beginner to make a fine copy of a favourite picture from a slide. For example, you can make a lovely icon on wood, and achieve a realistic 'antique' finish, or you can make a silhouette picture. Whatever subject you choose, you'll be delighted with the results.

Painting by projection

You don't have to be a Michelangelo or a Salvador Dali to paint successful pictures and designs. An easy, foolproof way is to choose a favourite slide and project it onto a surface. Then you can either paint it directly from the projected image or draw in the outline and paint in the image afterwards, making whatever changes and adaptations you wish within the basic outline. The slide projector technique can also be used for many other projects in the following pages, so it is useful to learn how to use it as soon as possible.

The projection technique has been used to get perspective right by many artists throughout the ages. The incredibly lifelike and decorative pictures of Vermeer, for instance, were sometimes outlined in this way, using the simplest form of projection, the *camera obscura*.

How projection works

The *camera obscura* refers to a natural phenomenon by which light coming into a dark room through a tiny aperture can cause a scene outside to be projected upside down onto a wall (fig. 1). (*Camera obscura* means 'dark room'.) By putting a lens into the aperture the image can be magnified and this is the principle of both the modern projector and the camera.

In the camera the light goes through a tiny aperture into a box where the image is projected onto light sensitive paper. In a projector the transparency is lit from behind and the image goes through the lens and is magnified on a wall or screen in a darkened room.

Subjects for projection

There is a wealth of material available on 35mm transparencies that can be either carefully copied and painted or simply outlined and used as a basis for improvisation. Most people have transparencies from their travels and many museums and galleries sell 35mm slides of items in their collections.

Images with bold, simple lines and flat colours with uncomplicated shading make excellent subjects. They are easier to sketch and fill in and are therefore best suited to projection technique.

Murals

One of the advantages of projection is that you can get a sizeable image, and for this reason it is especially useful for making murals. Niches, walls, even ceilings, can be decorated if you have enough distance to get very big images. In the case of large expanses such as ceilings, a repeated pattern or design can be projected to cover the area section by section.

The variety of subjects and styles is enormous. Slides of ancient Egyptian wall paintings, for instance, are numerous and these are excellent subjects since the outlines of figures and hieroglyphics are bold and simple and therefore easy to trace. An even more ambitious project would be to use slides of frescoes from Pompeii to decorate the walls of a dining room in the Roman style.

Early tapestries often have well-defined outlines and lend themselves extremely well to wall painting while the mural shown here is projected from a fifteenth-century manuscript illumination.

Other ways of making murals are shown later in the book.

Right: Slides of two illuminated pages from a fifteenth century manuscript were projected and painted in acrylic colours to make this double mural.

Below: The diagram illustrates how the diagonal behaviour of light makes projection possible.

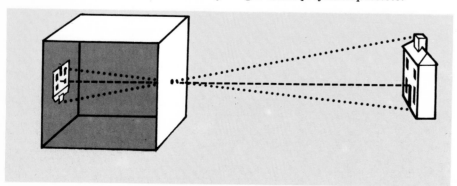

Pictures for framing

Not everyone wants to cover walls with painted images but people may, on the other hand, be happy to have framed pictures to hang on them. A projector is a satisfactory way to accomplish this, too, and successfully projected pictures can be made by copying existing works, and making reproductions of famous or lesser-known artists' work. Again, naive or primitive styles are most suited to this technique.

Copyright

If you intend to project images and sell the results, you must first find out about the copyright of the image you choose. If you have taken the photograph yourself, and it does not feature another person's design then you are free to use it. Otherwise, check the source of your chosen picture and find out if you can get permission to use it.

By using projection you are by no means limited to copying the work of others. Projection techniques can be as creative as they are decorative, and slides of real objects and of people can be transformed into paintings through projection. A photographic slide of a fruit bowl or table set for a meal is a good subject to begin with since the outlines of fruit, bottles and other objects are easily drawn yet can be used to develop an original oil painting like the one illustrated. Different objects can be rearranged to suit the design simply by moving or readjusting the projector.

Murals can also be made from 'live' guides made from photographs. Projected landscapes can be especially effective when painted in this way. A photograph of zoo animals or of the African bush with chubby zebras cropping grass, or tall giraffes nibbling the tops of acacia trees would make a delightful decoration on a nursery wall. A snapshot of a boat under full sail could be interpreted on canvas or painted to decorate an alcove. You need only to use your imagination.

Surfaces

Plaster walls are ideal but plain papered walls are also suitable for picture projection. Special effects can be achieved by using a textured wallpaper for the background. Make sure on papered walls, however, that the joins are very good or they may appear too prominently in the finished picture or, if loose, begin to peel later.

Pictures for framing can be projected onto hessian [burlap] mounted on wood, stretched canvas, hardboard, wood, chipboard [plywood] or paper – in fact, any surface that is flat and which will receive paint.

Roller blinds [window shades] are another good surface as their size is

generally right for receiving images projected from across an average-sized room.

Paints

Acrylic polymer paints are the best all-round materials for painting on walls or other surfaces. These are easy to use and come in a good range of colours. They can be diluted and cleaned up with water and you can buy what is known as an acrylic polymer reducing medium to give them transparency.

Above: It is possible to make 'original' paintings by projecting the shape and perspective of the subject onto canvas. This removes much of the difficulty of creating a picture from scratch.

Oil paints can of course be used for painting on canvas, and good quality artists' brushes are recommended for all surfaces.

For rough guidance only Standard lens 90mm using 35mm transparency		
Projector lens distance from wall	**Width of projected image**	**Height of projected image**
30cm (1ft)	9cm (3in)	5cm (2in)
61cm (2ft)	23cm (9in)	15cm (6in)
91cm (3ft)	34cm (13in)	22cm (8in)
1.22m (4ft)	46cm (18in)	30cm (12in)
1.52m (5ft)	58cm (23in)	38cm (15in)
1.83m (6ft)	71cm (28in)	46cm (18in)
2.13m (7ft)	78cm (31in)	51cm (20in)
2.44m (8ft)	91cm (36in)	59cm (23in)
3.66m (12ft)	1.42m (56ft)	91cm (36in)

Compact projector 70mm lens using 35mm transparency		
Projector lens distance from wall	**Width of projected image**	**Height of projected image**
30cm (1ft)	TOO CLOSE	
61cm (2ft)	27cm (10in)	16cm (7in)
91cm (3ft)	42cm (16in)	27cm (11in)
1.22m (4ft)	56cm (22in)	37cm (14in)
1.52m (5ft)	69cm (27in)	46cm (18in)
1.83m (6ft)	87cm (34in)	58cm (23in)
2.13m (7ft)	1.1m (40in)	67cm (26in)
2.44m (8ft)	1.17m (46in)	76cm (30in)
3.66m (12ft)	1.70m (67in)	1.4m (45in)

How to project

The chart gives a rough guide to the sizes of the images you can make projecting from various distances using a 35mm projector with 70mm or standard 90mm lenses. It is assumed that the whole transparency is to be used (you may, in some cases, only wish to use a part of the projected image).

Before you begin, make sure the surface is in good order; flaking plaster or old paint on walls must be scraped off and re-primed.

Line up the projector to fill the area of wall or canvas you want to paint. Remember that in order to see the full outline you must work in a darkened room, a *camera obscura*.

Turn on the projector and make any necessary adjustments in focus and height. Then, standing somewhat to the side of the image, begin to sketch in the outline with a soft pencil. Do not make the outline so prominent that it will be difficult to cover.

If you prefer to copy direct you can paint on top of the projected image. But you must keep turning off the projector to make sure your colours are covering properly and are the right shade and consistency.

You will find that in order to reach many areas of the image with your pencil or brush you must obscure other portions by standing in front of the projector and blocking the projection, but this presents few difficulties.

To fill in the outline, simply paint each area with the appropriate colour. For a convenient colour reference use either your transparency held to the light or, easier but more expensive, work from a colour print.

To protect the finished surfaces, especially walls which collect dust and must occasionally be washed, apply two coats of clear polyurethane varnish, which can be bought in either a matt or gloss finish.

Above left and right: The projected shapes are filled in on the canvas in pencil.

Below: The finished picture is still an 'original' even though short cuts were used.

Portraits from silhouettes

The art of the silhouette owes its name to an eighteenth-century French finance minister called Etienne de Silhouette, whose hobby was cutting out profiles in paper. Monsieur Silhouette and his unpopular tax reforms were soon forgotten but enthusiasm for the craft named after him has never waned.

Before the invention of photography the art of silhouette portraiture was particularly appreciated as a quick and simple method of getting a 'likeness', and there is hardly a museum in the world without an example of this craft, some exquisitely painted on plaster or ivory, some on card, others on glass backed with wax. But not all silhouettes were executed by artists. It was a pastime that could be enjoyed by anyone, and this of course remains true today.

Traditionally, silhouette portraits were made by drawing a profile freehand, or by casting a shadow in front of a candle onto a piece of paper, then reducing it with an apparatus called a pantograph. The shape was then filled in with black ink.

Today's methods are very mush the same, except that modern lighting produces better results. Use a clear, electric light bulb without a shade to project the shadow of the sitter in an otherwise darkened room. Better still, use a slide projector as a source of light if you have one. This will make the profile sharper and eliminate the second shadow which otherwise sometimes appears.

The light bulb method
You will need:
A sheet of thin white paper and a sheet of black or coloured cartridge [construction] paper. Alternatively a sheet of cartridge [construction] weight paper, black on one side, white on the reverse; drawing pins [thumbtacks]; a pencil or felt-tipped pen; sharp scissors; a slide projector or an unshaded electric light with clear bulb; a model and a chair.

Seat the model on the chair in a darkened room, as near the wall as possible, with his or her profile parallel to the wall.

Pin the paper to the wall directly behind the face (white side uppermost if two-toned paper is used).

Position the light on the other side of the face, adjusting it until the shadow falls sharply onto the paper.

Above: A delightful example of a silhouette from the eighteenth century, this picture is painted on flat glass.

Below: The diagram illustrates the light bulb method of making a silhouette. It is very simple to do.

Trace the profile of the face and head onto the paper with pencil or felt-tipped pen.

If you have used two-tone paper, simply cut along your pencilled lines, turn the paper over and your silhouette is ready.

If you have used plain white paper, trace the profile onto black or coloured paper of your choice, and cut it out.

To reduce or enlarge a silhouette

If the accuracy of the light bulb method appeals to you but you want the end result to be a small silhouette, you can use the light bulb technique to trace the sitter's profile and reduce the silhouette afterwards. It is also possible to enlarge a small picture, such as a

profile snapshot, to make a large silhouette. For this you can either use the reducing and enlarging technique described next, or a pantograph.

To enlarge a design, trace it onto tracing paper (fig. 1). Lay this over graph paper. If you can see the squares clearly through the tracing paper, stick it down with clear adhesive tape, being careful that the tracing paper lies flat. This way, you can re-use the graph paper.

If, however, you cannot see the squares clearly, transfer the design to the graph paper either with carbon paper (dressmaker's carbon is fine) or by shading the back of the tracing paper with a soft pencil and drawing firmly over the design with a ballpoint.

Draw a rectangle to enclose the

Below: A small profile snapshot is simultaneously traced and enlarged by a pantograph. The instrument is screwed to a flat surface, and masking tape is used to prevent original and copy paper from slipping. Adjustable central screws are set in holes numbered '3' because original is to be enlarged three times. As one hand guides tracer (BD) along lines to be copied, the other lightly holds pencil lead (C) and enlarged reproduction appears on the copy paper. If the image were to be made smaller, the pantograph could be reassembled to reverse the procedure.

design (fig. 2). If you are using plain paper you must divide the rectangle up by marking off each side and joining the marks to make squares. It is helpful to number these for reference.

Next, draw a second rectangle, preferably on tracing paper as before, to the size you want the finished design to be and in the same proportions as the first one. Do this by tracing two adjacent sides of the first rectangle and the diagonal from where they meet. Extend them as much as you need and then draw in the other sides of the second rectangle (fig. 3). Divide this into the same number of squares as the smaller one. A backing sheet of graph paper will make this process easier.

Carefully copy the design square by square. If you have to copy a flowing, curved line across several squares, mark the points at which it crosses the squares and then join them up in one flowing movement (fig. 4).

To reduce a design, simply reverse the process as given here. This method of enlarging or reducing can be used for many purposes and is referred to in some of the other projects in this book.

Using a pantograph

A pantograph is an adjustable wooden or plastic instrument, available from art stores, for mechanical copying on a reduced or enlarged scale. As the tracer is drawn along the lines to be copied, a lead simultaneously reproduces them in a reduced (or enlarged) form. The scale of reproduction is determined by placing central screws in numbered holes, and the positioning of tracer and lead determines whether the original is to be reduced or enlarged.

The window method

This is another way to make a silhouette which produces a smaller portrait than is possible using the light bulb technique. It must be pointed out, however, that you need a good eye to get really accurate results with this method. You have to draw the profile rather than simply trace the shadow, and the further away the model, the greater the challenge.

You will need:

A ground floor window; a sheet of cellophane paper; a felt-tipped pen; transparent adhesive tape and a model

Place the sheet of cellophane over the inside of the window glass and secure it with transparent tape.

Stand your model out of doors, in profile on the other side of the window. To get the silhouette the correct size, ask the model to move back until his or her head is the desired size. Then trace the silhouette onto the cellophane with felt-tipped pen.

Trace onto coloured paper and cut out as described above.

If you don't have a ground floor window, buy an old picture frame from a junk shop, or make a wood and glass or Perspex [Plexiglass] frame (fig. 5). Then make the silhouette in a large room, following the procedures described above.

Original ideas

Don't feel bound to use only the traditional black and white silhouette papers. Extremely interesting variations can be made using coloured papers of your choice. And there is no reason to restrict yourself to head and shoulder portraits. Silhouettes can be made of hand shapes, bowls of flowers, or fruit, or combined with collage costumes, or almost anything you like.

Have fun, too, with the way you use your silhouettes. Instead of framing them singly in the conventional way, mount two heads face to face on a heart-shaped background; make silhouettes of all the family and put them in one frame.

Below: How to enlarge an image using graph paper.
1. Draw design on tracing paper.
2. Lay tracing paper over graph paper, draw rectangle, and number squares. 3. Draw second rectangle by tracing two sides and a diagonal from first, extend as needed. 4. Transfer the design square by square.
5. Frame for use indoors.

Opposite: Use ribbons and lace to decorate silhouettes, and give them a period touch.

Your own antique icon

Icons were first produced during the period of Byzantine art which stretched from about the eleventh to the fifteenth century. Their significance was religious rather than artistic; but the craftsmen who produced them were highly trained in the techniques of their day.

The painting of an icon was usually on a wooden panel constructed of two or three smaller pieces joined together by a frame. The whole of this panel was first coated with a kind of plaster called *gesso* before work commenced in paint.

In recent times icons have become highly valued works of art, especially in western countries where they change hands at very high prices. This is partly because they were only produced in Eastern Europe and Asia Minor, and also because of their antiquity. It is the last point that probably gives them a particular appeal, lending them an air of timelessness and magic.

To make a modern icon

You can find illustrations of icons in many reference books on art, and by following the method described here produce something which looks very like the real thing. You do not need the drawing skills of a great artist since it is possible to transfer the image by tracing or produce an enlarged image by using a slide projector. Many museums and galleries have slides of icons for sale and it is also possible to have a slide made by taking a picture of an icon in a book.

You will need:

Slide projector or tracing materials; selection of artist's brushes; spatula or other implement for spreading; light-weight hammer; one piece of 6mm ($\frac{1}{4}$in) plywood about 23cm by 38cm (9in by 1ft 3in) or size of your choice; 1.2m (4ft) of 2.5cm (1in) wide rounded beading (or to fit chosen plywood); small packet of patching plaster [small container of vinyl spackling compound]; 1cm ($\frac{3}{8}$in) panel pins [slim nails]; small tin ordinary wood varnish; waterproof inks in colours such as the following: white, black, green, scarlet, ultramarine, yellow, burnt sienna and nut brown.

Preparing the surface

Before starting on your icon, it is well to bear in mind that you are attempting to make a painting that has a feeling of age about it. Therefore you will need to take special care from the start to build this into the picture. On the wooden panels that were made long ago, humidity and temperature changes have often caused the wood strips to expand and contract, thereby stressing the paint along their lengths. This is a characteristic of real icons, so you may like to reproduce it accordingly.

Saw your piece of plywood into three strips about 7.5cm (3in) wide.

Cut the beading (or have it cut) into lengths that will make a frame around the three strips when they are laid into a panel (fig. 1). Beading can be mitred; but this is not essential.

Nail the beading to the plywood with the panel pins [slim nails], and use a

14

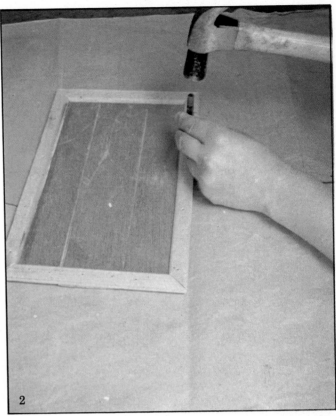

1

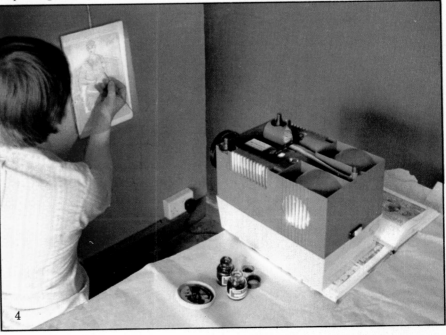

2

Opposite: How old is this icon? It really does look authentic. Make it yourself, following the instructions given in this chapter.

Figs. 1-4 on this page show the preparation of icon base, and the use of the projector to cast the image. If you wish to use this image, you can trace it from the pattern given on page 17.

punch to bury the pins just beneath the beading surface (fig. 2).

Having completed this stage mix a quantity of plaster into a creamy paste [or use the ready-mixed spackling] – the mixture should be the same consistency as icing for a cake.

With a kitchen spatula, or similar utensil, spread the mixture evenly over the front of the panel and its beading frame. Do not forget about the edges and avoid a smooth finish – the slight roughness of the surface will further help to 'age' the paintwork (fig. 3).

Now place the plastered panel in a very hot oven and leave for about fifteen minutes to dry. This will make the plaster crack slightly in the same way that age would crack paintwork.

Painting the image

You are now ready to begin tracing out the icon that you have selected from an illustration. If you are using a projector the panel should be hung on a convenient wall space and the projector placed so that the image is not distorted (fig. 4). The example shown

3

4

5

6

7

projected here can be traced from the sketch shown either in the size shown or enlarged to its original size of 23cm by 38cm (9in by 3in).

When you project an image you can paint the outline directly onto the prepared board. When tracing, pencil it lightly before beginning (fig. 5).

Mix up a little nut brown ink on an old saucer and with a fine brush start to paint in the main lines of the composition. A simple coloured outline is all that is required at this stage, so do not worry about adding too much detail. Using your drawing inks, paint in all the main washes of colour in flat tones. The uneven plaster surface will already begin to give your paint an authentic appearance (fig. 6).

Take extra care with the background colour. Usually yellow ink, or nut

brown thinned a little with water, is most effective if followed by a rough wash of grey or light green on top. Do not use bright colours.

Work up all the shading and highlights (fig. 7); but remember that icons were painted in a very flat style, so too much realism is not required. Make sure that you also add lettering.

Distressing the surface

When your painting is complete then it is the time to start the final 'ageing' process. To do this you should not be afraid to be a bit ruthless – real icons have survived for centuries.

First take the panel between your two hands, holding it at its extreme edges. With your fingers press gently upwards on the underside and along the joins in the three wood strips (fig.

8). The surface of the paintwork should then crack along these lines; but do not allow too many large pieces of plaster to fall away.

Lay the icon back on the table and replace one or two loose pieces of paintwork roughly in their original positions. Now carefully varnish the surface, allowing the varnish to stick loose pieces into place (fig. 9), and leave to dry.

The picture should now be blackened a little by holding it over the tip of a naked flame. Your icon is now finished and is ready to be hung.

Figs 5-9 describe how to paint and then distress the surface to 'age' it.

Opposite: Trace off this sketch.

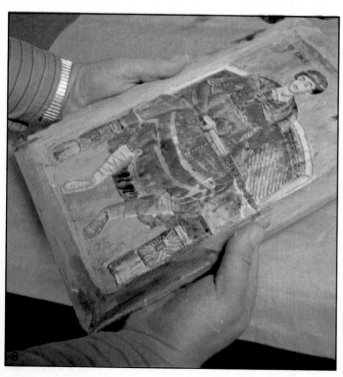

8

9

17

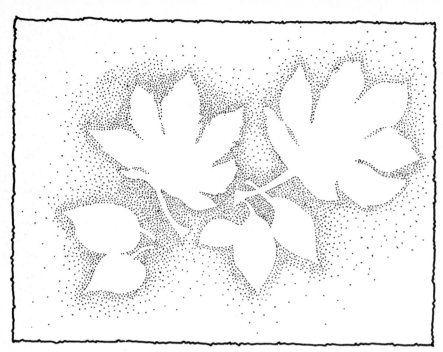

Pictures with paints

You don't have to be a trained artist to paint an original picture which looks completely professional. Many people are deterred from experimenting with paint because they feel that it has a special mystique. In fact, new design discoveries such as the technique for making an 'instant' abstract painting have released an enormous amount of inspiration and ingenuity. The pleasure of using colour in a free and spontaneous way, while at the same time achieving a really authoritative look is available to anyone. Once you have tried a few variations with spatter painting for example, and have appreciated the range of tones and effects you can obtain, you'll want to make lots of pictures. In addition, for those who have always admired hand-tinted prints, we show you how to colour your own at home, and with really subtle, authentic results that you'll be proud to display.

Instant abstract painting

Ever since the invention of the camera artists have moved further and further from representational painting, increasingly exploring new shapes and forms and new ways of making them. They have applied paint with their hands, walked and rolled over their canvases, dribbled paint from a tube and thrown colours at canvas like custard pies. And while this has caused some scepticism from the average person it has often elicited admiration from the experts.

One of the easiest ways of exploring colour and form is also one of the most enjoyable. It was developed at the Jaeger display studios and involves dropping French enamel varnish and methylated spirit [de-natured alcohol] onto a sheet of PVC. Within a few minutes you have an abstract painting with the fascinating luminosity that is peculiar to enamel varnish.

The success of your picture will depend entirely on your choice of colour and the way you choose to manipulate it on the 'canvas'.

The basic materials

French enamel varnish is a traditional material for painting and finishing furniture, but it has been to some extent replaced by polyurethane. However, it can still be bought in a number of different colours and quantities, and although most paint and hardware shops may not stock it your local furniture restorer should be able to supply you or tell you who will. This type of painting can also be done with drawing inks, but the effect is not nearly so good since the colours do not run as well as varnish.

PVC (polyvinyl chloride) is a shiny plastic sheeting which can be bought by the metre (yard). Although white is the most useful colour for painting, other shades are available too. The width is usually 130cm (51in). The paint should go on the glossier side.

Hardboard painted with vinyl emulsion paint can also be used if you find PVC difficult to obtain, but it is not quite as effective as PVC.

Methylated spirit [de-natured alcohol], the final ingredient in this method, can be bought in any hardware shop. It is a solvent for enamel varnish and its purpose is to dilute the varnish on the 'canvas' and encourage it to run.

Preparing the surface

Before you begin to paint you must mount the PVC on a sturdy backing. Hardboard makes the quickest and most inexpensive mount. Just stretch the PVC across it, folding the edges over and stapling them to the back of the board with a staple gun (fig. 1). Alternatively you can mount it on 6mm (¼in) plywood.

For a stretched canvas look make a wooden frame the intended size of your picture with 5cm by 2.5cm (2in by 1in) width wood and nail the hardboard to the wood frame. Then stretch the PVC tightly across this backing and staple it to the underside of the stretcher frame (fig. 2).

Large pictures lend themselves best to this kind of painting since considerable space is needed to obtain the right effect.

The overall size of pictures is limited somewhat by the width of the PVC. In addition, you should allow at least 2.5cm (1in) at each edge for folding over hardboard and just over 5cm (2in) for stretching over hardboard and stretcher frame.

Working area

Painting of this kind is best carried out in a garage, basement or other area where the surroundings will not be harmed by accidental splashing of the colour. Alternatively, cover the working area with old newspapers, and wear old clothes or overalls.

The floor is the best place to put your 'canvas' but you can also use a table. It is very important that it lies absolutely flat or the colour will all run in one direction when applied.

Painting

The trick of enamel varnish painting is to drop the varnish on the PVC and get it to spread in an interesting and pleasing pattern. To do this you should position yourself some distance from the PVC – sufficiently far for the paints to splash. Stooping down beside the PVC and pouring the varnish out of the bottle about a forearm's length above the 'canvas' gives you the most control, but interesting effects can be made by standing up over the surface too. The more dramatic painters even work from ladders.

To begin, pour a pool of methylated spirit [de-natured alcohol] onto the centre of the PVC. Next pour on a little colour, either making a puddle or moving the bottle around. It is advisable to start with a light colour first, otherwise the results may look muddy. Now add another colour, then add some more methylated spirit [de-natured alcohol], and then perhaps another colour. Repeat up to about three colours.

The amount of methylated spirit [de-natured alcohol] you use will be several times that of varnish. If you have put too much on, dab it up with a paper towel. You can also begin by putting varnish on first and then methylated spirit [de-natured alcohol].

Special effects

There are several ways to get different effects and no doubt you will invent a few of your own once you have mastered the basic technique of using varnish and spirit [alcohol].

Tipping the board slightly at the corner will make the colours slide in

Fig. 1 shows PVC stretched over hardboard and then stapled to the back.
Fig. 2 shows hardboard nailed to a wooden frame and PVC stretched across.

the opposite direction.

A decorator's paintbrush can be used to flick or shake spirit [alcohol] onto the PVC. You can also drag your brush across the surface, but if you wish to leave a squiggle or other brush trail on the PVC then wait until the varnish has begun to dry.

Masking tape or contact paper will protect parts of the painting surface and can be used to make a border on the 'canvas'.

Stencils can be cut from contact paper or other material with a light adhesive backing and applied to the PVC. For instance, a huge butterfly motif could be used, the glossy, rainbow effect of the varnish making its glimmering wings.

Below: The picture over the couch looks like an expensive abstract painting by an avant garde artist. It has a fascinating luminous effect, which contributes towards its atmosphere of drama and mystery. In fact it was made very quickly and inexpensively by pouring French enamel varnish and methylated spirits [de-natured alcohol] onto a sheet of gleaming PVC material.

Above: Pour methylated spirit [de-natured alcohol] on canvas.

Above: Next pour out some French enamel varnish.

Above: Shake brushful of spirit to make tiny splashes.

Above: You can make splashes with your hands as well.

Spatter painting

Spatter painting means just what the name suggests – splashing or spattering paint. By simply laying a shape such as a leaf or cut-out design on a sheet of paper and flicking colour on it from a stiff brush, paint or ink builds up around the marked off area and the shape remains as a kind of silhouette when the design is removed (fig. 1). The surrounding area has the textured, speckled effect that spattering gives.

While a stiff brush is the traditional tool for spatter painting the development of the aerosol has considerably enlarged the type of designs and surfaces possible. The traditional methods are much more satisfying however and give a greater variety of styles.

Designs

Whatever the surface you are decorating make sure your subject or design is suited to spatter techniques which are, in effect, silhouette techniques. Detailed or complicated motifs will end up as a confused mess. Keep your design simple and do not use too many colours.

Leaves and ferns are very popular design images for spatter painting but they must be pressed first so that they will lie flat on the surface being spattered.

Children find spattering simple cut-outs an easy and enjoyable pastime while adults can use the technique to make more intricate decorations on lampshades, clothing and household linen and decor.

Materials

These are very simple and easy to get. The colour medium you choose depends on the surface you are spattering. On paper, watercolours are perfectly suitable and, since they are washable, are recommended for children. Ink can also be used but, again, a washable type is recommended since there is always the danger of spots getting flicked on clothing or nearby furniture.

Cold water fabric dyes work well on fabrics and are colour fast. Prepare the dye according to the manufacturer's instructions and then use it as you would use paint.

Cartridge [construction] paper and any other slightly absorbent paper is suitable for spattering. A coated surface may cause the colour to run and so impair the finely dotted effect distinctive to the technique. Fabrics should be natural fibres such as cotton or linen, though you can use viscose rayon as an option.

Use an old toothbrush or a nailbrush. It is important that the bristles are reasonably stiff so that they have enough spring to throw the paint when they are flicked. An old dinner knife can be used to flick the paint covered bristles or you can use fingers.

How to spatter

Protect the area you are working in by putting down newspapers and wearing old clothes or overalls.

Put some colour in a saucer and load your brush by dipping it.

Hold the brush over the printing surface with bristle side up and either draw the blade of a dinner knife briskly toward you across the bristles of the brush or use your finger in the same manner. (Although the latter is rather messy and not recommended for dyes, it is advisable for small children.) The action of the blade or finger being pulled across the brush causes the paint to spatter as the bristles are released and jump back into place.

With practice it is quite easy to control direction and density of the colour. Blobs are to be avoided but do not expect all the spots of paint to be the same size. The different sizes add visual interest to the surface.

Using a diffuser

A less messy way to spatter is with a diffuser. This is a simple device made of two tubes. You blow through one and the other syphons the ink and spatters the surface. Colour is easier to control and the gadget is not expensive and can be purchased at most art supply shops.

A diffuser is especially recommended for spatter painting on fabrics with dyes since the fine, even spray produced gives a more professional finish.

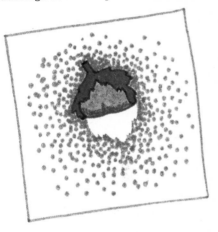

Above: Spatter painting is a silhouette technique. When the image is lifted off its outline remains.

Below and overleaf: The misty outlines of these ferns, and the variety of subtle effects in the collection of examples overleaf show just how exciting spatter painting can be.

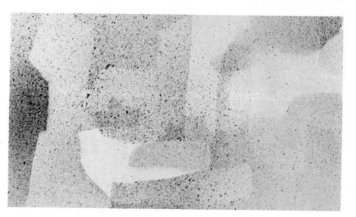

Hand tinting prints

Almost any uncoloured print can be made considerably more attractive by the addition of colour artistically applied. Since prints already have their subjects fully drawn, adding colour is an easy way for beginners to learn something about the use of colour and painting techniques in general.

History of tinted engravings

Nowadays meticulous hand-tinting of old engravings is only practised by a specialized few, but during the eighteenth and nineteenth centuries, publishers and print-sellers flourished with public demand for pictures; labour was cheap and attempts at producing quality art inexpensively resulted in the hand-colouring of monochrome prints. In the 1830s hand-colouring was the cheapest method of producing coloured prints, and lithographs were still being coloured by hand in the 1860s. Many subsequently famous artists, such as Turner, began their careers in this way, acquiring basic skill in handling brush and colour in the publishers' workrooms.

Between 1812 and 1821 there were also many penniless aristocratic refugees from the French Revolution only too happy to earn a few coins by colouring prints.

Some systems were more repetitive than creative, however. Artists would etch the original outlines on the copper plate and some would then colour a sample print in pale washes to be copied in quantity. The workers, many of them children, sat in a circle; each had a colour allotted to him, and brushed it on wherever it appeared in the guide copy; then he passed it to his neighbour for the next colour to be added. An edition of a book with many plates might require the hand-colouring of some 10,000 prints.

Obtaining engravings for tinting

Print shops and second-hand book-sellers are the best source of black and white engravings. These are often inexpensive and usually in reasonably good condition.

If you wish to find out what colouring prints would have had if they had been tinted when published, a trip to the local library and antique print-sellers will be helpful. Museums are another place to find antique prints. You will be able to find some good reproductions in museum shops.

Preparation

Before colouring old engravings it is usually necessary to clean off the grime of a century or more.

Dry cleaning of loose surface dirt can be done with a ball of soft, slightly moist bread. A very soft eraser can be gently used on the margins and back, but never on the engraved surface.

Removing blemishes

Few antique prints will be completely free from the brown spots or blemishes known as 'foxing'. These are caused by exposure to pollution, smoke, damp, food crumbs, etc., and must be removed by bleaching. Immerse the print in a shallow solution of sodium hydrochloride or common household bleach, diluted with water to the volume of one part bleach to 20 parts water. This is a very strong, quick acting solution; a print will need between one and three minutes immersion to clean all but the heaviest foxing. Remember that when the print is wet it is very fragile, and any unsupported tugging will tear it. Rinse the print gently in clean water before leaving to dry.

Above: Making a collection of hand-tinted prints is an inexpensive way of adding a 'connoisseur's touch'.

Opposite: A wide variety of effects can be achieved with spatter painting techniques.

Sizing

After drying, the print must be thoroughly sized to restore the strength of the paper, and to render it waterproof, so that traces of colour do not penetrate to the back.

Bottles of prepared size in jelly form can be bought in most art supply shops. This must be dissolved in warm water, one part of size to three of water by volume.

Alternatively, dissolve ¼ teaspoon of household gelatine in a litre (1¾ pints) [4½ cups] of hot water, and use immediately, brushing the solution across the surface of the print in broad flat strokes but only in one direction.

Colouring

To start colouring, practise on a print of little value. Use three or four good-quality sable or camel-hair brushes ranging from sizes 2 to 4, for small octavo-sized prints and sizes 8 to 10 for large folio prints.

Keep to simple basic watercolours – indigo, Prussian blue, ultramarine, sepia, sienna, umber, light red, gamboge, ochre, olive green, viridian, Payne's grey, Naples yellow and a tube of Chinese white (opaque).

Acrylic white gesso is also useful for underpainting highlights, such as on silk dresses which, when dry, can have transparent colour laid over it with great effect. This is also a good way of outlining a dark figure against a dark background.

Begin colouring at the top of the print – the sky, if there is one.

Mix Prussian blue with white or ultramarine very well diluted. It is much better to use very weak washes in the initial stages than to inadvertently use too strong a tone, which cannot be washed out. Remember you can always add more strength later if required, but cannot take it away. Try to finish a sky in one wash.

If you want to merge a pink cloud against a hazy blue background, first dampen the area with clean water before using a mixture of raw sienna, light red and white. Naples yellow is also useful in skies.

Always remember that most of the toning work has already been done for you by the engraver and that only flat washes of colour are required.

In a landscape keep your middle section and horizon as cool in colour as possible; use blues, greys and lavender, to obtain recession. Keep the warm tones, burnt sienna, ochre and light red for the bottom foreground. Do not waste your light areas by killing them with an opaque colour; keep them light with pretty transparent colours. Save the opaque colours for the dark details, highlighted with tiny touches of Chinese white.

Buildings are pale washes of raw umber or ochre, brick is light red, slate roofs are payne's grey, cupolas, lime green.

Trees in the foreground are olive green lightened with ochre or gamboge, blueing to payne's grey and viridian in the distance.

Shadowed areas can be cool with blues, or warm with mauve or burnt sienna.

Figures and vehicles

Leave these until last. Bright spots of colour for mail coaches and carts, young ladies' dresses in light pinks and blues, older people in darker, more sedate colours.

Flesh tints are obtained by well-diluted light red with a touch of Naples yellow, or for a more ruddy peasant complexion mix with burnt sienna for a truly authentic effect.

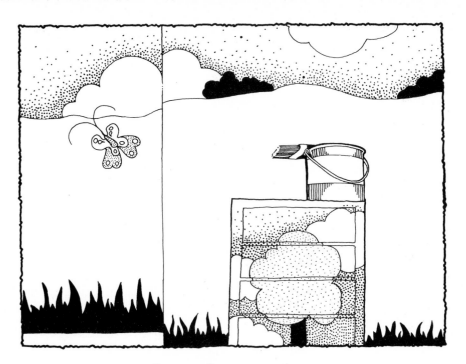

Murals

Murals can be painted on any wall you choose, although they are mainly features of bathrooms, halls and childrens' rooms. The concept of painting large-scale landscapes directly onto an interior wall is very ancient indeed—the Greeks and Romans were certainly very fond of this kind of decoration, and the remains of the ruined city of Pompeii show some really gorgeous examples, with a wide range of styles. A quiet browse through some books with good illustrations of buildings from ancient cultures will indicate the variety of pictorial subjects used to transform plain walls into exciting vistas. The projector technique described in the first chapter is an ideal method for casting a large-scale image, and the following projects give some further methods and ideas. Any child would love a pastoral scene with delightful animals roaming across his wall, or perhaps a favourite pet could be used as a central theme. Whatever subject you choose, you'll be delighted with method of combining the craft of picture making with creative interior decoration.

Bathroom mural

A brightly coloured mural is the ideal way to decorate an unexciting bathroom and it can be surprisingly inexpensive and simple to do.

Apart from the background colours which will probably take quite a lot of paint, depending on the area of your walls, you may find that you can economize on the smaller amounts needed by using up paint left over from decorating projects. If you are buying paint, choose a non-drip emulsion which goes on with a good coverage, so you will not have to go over the shapes twice. You will also need a selection of various sized paint brushes, plus some transparent varnish specially made for use in bathrooms to resist marks and condensation.

The design shown in the photograph looks quite elaborate, but apart from the frog and the butterfly all the shapes are simple. The flowers are stylized and can easily be drawn with the aid of a stencil, and the rushes are simply brush strokes, as are the clouds.

If you feel the whole design is rather ambitious for you, start with the background and fill in with a few flowers and rushes. If these are successful it is a simple matter to add more to them. Mistakes can be wiped off while the paint is still wet or covered with emulsion paint if dry. Always allow the coats to dry before using another colour next to them.

Making a stencil
Trace over the required shape and then place the tracing over cardboard with carbon paper, shiny side down, between the two.

Trace over the shape again to transfer it to the cardboard. Cut out the shape from the cardboard.

Preparing the walls
If your walls are papered, strip them and make good any cracks with cellulose filler. If the walls are painted with gloss paint either strip them or cover with lining paper.

Coat the wall with a matt wall sealer.

Painting the design
Start by painting in the blue sky of the background. Allow to dry.

Paint in the white clouds, being careful to curve the edges with the brush. Allow to dry.

Paint in the hills and the other parts of the background.

Using the stencil and a light pencil sketch on the flowers, the butterfly and the frog then fill in with paint.

Paint in the rushes and add any finishing touches. Allow to dry.

Coat the finished design with a special transparent varnish for bathrooms.

Left: Have fun and brighten up your bathroom with this evocative scene of the banks of a pool in summer.

Right: Shapes for stencils.

26

Painting scenic murals

The earliest pictures in houses were murals or frescoes painted directly onto walls to give the impression of exterior views seen through falso windows and doorways. In fact, the word *alfresco* means 'outdoors'.

Today it is possible to create similar illusions but these can be accomplished using simpler techniques both in design and application than were used by craftsmen of the past.

Designing murals

The chief effect of scenic murals is to alter the spatial effect of a room by 'opening it up' but several factors must be considered before proceeding to paint one.

The space available is a prime consideration. A mural might occupy a small alcove, an entire wall or ceiling or it might be extended to include the whole room as in the nursery mural shown. Doors and window frames could also be incorporated into the design.

The scale of the images is also very important and must be planned in relation to the height of the room. The placement of windows, doors and furniture must also be borne in mind. Therefore, always plan the design to scale on paper first so that the finished mural will fit the space allotted and the proportions of images will be suitable to those of the room.

Another important consideration is the use of the room involved and its existing mood. Obviously a Chinese garden with a pagoda would not be appropriate on the wall of a rustic cottage.

Transferring the design

Traditionally, frescoes were applied to damp plaster so that paint and plaster mixed together for greater durability. The design was sketched first on paper and each section enlarged to the appropriate size, then tiny prick marks were made on the paper with a pointed instrument along the sketch lines. Next each section was held in position against the wall and charcoal was rubbed through the holes to register the guidelines.

Happily, there are less complex methods of applying wall designs today while assuring a degree of longevity.

Sketches and tracings are still necessary however. Initially, tracings can be made from scenes in books or simple sketches can be drawn freehand and then be enlarged to the appropriate

size as shown in previous chapters. To transfer the design cut out the enlarged sections, then hold them in place against the wall and draw around them

Above and opposite: Every child will love these funny animals grazing and playing in a nursery scenic mural.

with a light pencil or coloured chalk.

The projection method

Projection is another useful method if the subject is chosen from a transparency. Slide projectors automatically enlarge an image. The outline can then be sketched for filling in later or the scene can be painted on the wall directly as it is projected. This technique is described in detail in the section on page 6.

Finally, you can always use freehand drawing. Simple images are the easiest to work with and, using coloured chalk, any details can be re-sketched and to some extent rubbed out. For primitive or naive subjects, such as the nursery mural shown, a certain amount of freehand sketching is an advantage.

Paint

Although enamel paints are the most durable wall finishes they are difficult to use because they are inclined to drip. Therefore water-based or emulsion paints are preferable.

When designing a mural, it is worth choosing colours which are readily available in emulsion form in the quantities you require. Emulsion paints can also be mixed to produce subtle shading or an altogether different hue.

Preparing and protecting the surface

Always make sure that the area to be painted is in proper condition to receive paint. Repair and prime any flaking paint or plaster (new plaster must always be primed before paint is applied) and wash the wall, if it has not

been recently painted, so that all grime is removed. It is normally advisable to start with a white base so that any colours applied to the wall will not be affected by the tone underneath.

To protect the surface of the mural when completed, two coats of polyurethane varnish can be applied in matt or gloss finish.

Nursery mural

Waking up to blue skies and green fields is undeniably pleasant and the simplicity of the landscape in this design makes it possible to reproduce without much skill.

The design must be adapted to the size and shape of the room to be painted and the animals and trees arranged accordingly. Therefore sketch the design to a smaller scale on paper first, arranging or rearranging the figures to suit the particular room.

It may also be a help to enlarge and cut out the animal shapes and experiment with their arrangement by taping them in different locations in the room.

Outlining the design

Use coloured chalk and begin by drawing a line which will divide the grass and sky. Do this freehand since an undulating line is required. Note that to repeat the scale of the mural shown the line should be drawn to make about two-thirds of the wall represent grass and one-third represent sky.

The clouds should be outlined next by drawing around plates and saucers pressed alternately against the wall (and ceiling) to get the fluffy curves characteristic of clouds. Observe the

effective way in which some clouds in the room shown are painted half on the ceiling and half on the wall to increase the three-dimensional feeling of the sky overhead.

Next sketch in freehand a few small, rounded bushes on the horizon and add the simplified large trees in the foreground in the same way. Then, having enlarged and cut out the outlines of the animals and flowers, position the patterns to the wall in the desired places and draw around.

Again, use a little ingenuity to give each sheep an individual ruffle in his coat. The more freehand drawing used throughout the better the result.

When arranging the figures be sure to make an allowance for the grass border along the skirting board which will be painted later.

Painting

Begin with the blue sky, taking as much care as possible not to overlap onto the cloud areas. Two coats will doubtless be required throughout but if you are careful the clouds can remain the white background colour of the wall and will not have to be repainted.

When the sky is dry, begin to paint the fields, again avoiding as far as possible painting over the sketches of the figures. Tree trunks and animals can come next. Use artists' brushes for fine details.

Finally, using a darker shade of green, fill in the bushes on the horizon and proceed to paint the baseboard. When this is done, add the vertical grass blades freehand.

Collage
pictures

Collage is an ideal technique for today's world—it makes use of the unwanted objects of our consumer society, which discards as quickly as it acquires. There is something inherently satisfying in making creative use of surplus ephemera, and many of the world's greatest artists including Picasso, Matisse and Braque have created lovely collages. One of the most exciting features of collage pictures is the range of textures and densities that can be achieved starting from a flat surface. It is possible to create a three-dimensional effect if you are cunning enough to place objects in the right juxtaposition to one another. You can make collage pictures from literally anything—yarns, fabrics, paper, scraps of fabric, pieces of metal are just a few examples, and you can choose a wide range of effects from the very realistic to the wildly fanciful. Once you've got the general idea, you'll look at everyday objects with a fresh eye, and have the thrill of re-cycling leftover bits and pieces into unique works of art.

Paper collage pictures

The word collage (derived from the French verb *coller* meaning to glue) is used to describe the abstract art form of juxtaposing and gluing together different materials to create a picture. Of all picture-making techniques, collage is probably the most versatile – and therefore of universal appeal to adults and children alike.

It is simple and great fun to do. Gluing requires no particular skill, and it is utterly absorbing to see the various effects that can be achieved by relating materials of differing texture, shape, colour and pattern.

Compositions can be as straightforward or as intricate as you wish; they can be flat or three-dimensional, and you can use more or less whatever materials you care to choose – from used matchsticks to egg cartons – so just let your imagination run riot.

Paper collage is, of course, restricted to using paper materials only. This makes it more manageable than some other types of collage, and costs are negligible if you use papers to be found in the home – but don't be misled into thinking this means it is any the less enjoyable or creative.

In fact, paper collage provides a particularly fascinating and challenging exercise – because it is only when you start a serious search that you become aware of just how rich and varied is the choice of papers available. And it's only when you start combining them that you realize the almost infinite variety of effects that can be achieved.

Papers in the home

Just go into the kitchen, see how many different papers you can find here – and you may well come to the conclusion that there's no need to go out and buy special papers for making a collage!

Probably you will find a thick brown paper bag or, perhaps, a prettily decorated one; absorbent paper towels; semi-transparent grease-proof paper; gleaming cooking foil; labels in decorative shapes and colours on jam jars, cheese boxes, tinned foods and soft drink bottles; lacy paper doilies; cereal cartons and other packets in thin cardboard.

The living room will yield still more. Old picture postcards, perhaps with foreign stamps, thick writing paper and flimsy airmail paper (coloured, ruled or plain), envelopes of various shapes,

sizes and colours, brown wrapping papers, corrugated paper, blotting paper, shiny sweet [candy] and chocolate wrappers, garden seed packets, bus, train, theatre and old air tickets, an invitation card, cheque book stubs, receipts from stores, old photographs and negatives, leftover pieces of wallpaper, cigarette packets and gold backed cigarette packet lining paper, paper napkins and of course, magazines and newspapers.

As you can see, the choice of papers is huge. And it is quite extraordinary how many and varied are the effects that can be achieved depending on the way papers are combined.

Using colour, texture and shape

Experiment with a square each of thin white cardboard, scarlet tissue and kitchen silver foil. See how many different correlations of texture, colour and pattern can be made with only these three papers.

For instance, a geometric pattern with the squares laid side by side and

Above: Choosing and cutting out suitable material from magazines can be enjoyed by all the family. Use paper trays to sort and classify the different kinds.

Opposite: Your own gallery of attractively framed collage pictures.

just overlapping will show each colour alone, their interaction and changes where they overlap.

Accentuate the different textures by sprinkling the tissue with a little water and rubbing it with a cloth so that it has a delicate streaked sunset look, and fringe the foil like a gleaming flowing mane or waving grasses.

Use the papers for three dimensional movement, rolling the card like a log and wrapping it with superimposed layers of foil and tissue cut into flame shapes. Or cup the tissue into giant poppy shapes and scratch the foil to make veined leaves. The permutations are almost endless.

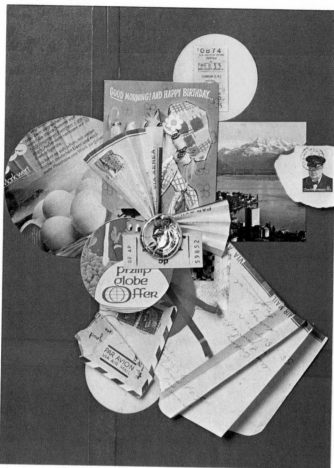

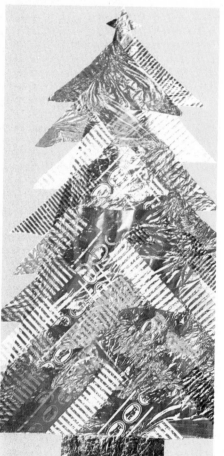

Collecting special papers

It is fun to collect papers with a particular project in mind. For instance, you might search out and put to one side papers of the same colour tone, seeing just how many different textures and patterns there are. You might choose a subject and search out as many different visual interpretations of it as you can find. Or, on holiday, you might collect postcards, a menu, your tickets, the label from a local wine, a theatre programme and a local newspaper to form the basis of a nostalgic holiday memento collage.

But there is no need to collect vast quantities of different papers before embarking on a project of this sort. Most collages are simply creations of the moment and should be enjoyed as such. The Christmas tree collage illustrated here is made entirely from sweet [candy] papers – and serves as an excellent example.

To make a paper collage
You will need:

Stiff cardboard, hardboard or plywood of required finished size for mounting the collage; papers; scissors. A rubber-based adhesive such as Cow Gum [Elmer's Glue All]; a clear general purpose glue; hardboard or plywood off-cuts can often be bought cheaply from do-it-yourself shops.

Use rubber based adhesive for papers which are to be stuck flat, and the stronger, clear, general purpose glue for three-dimensional effects when only part of a piece of paper is to be glued onto the mount. Always spread glue in a thin even coat as this adheres more effectively and is less likely to mark papers than large blobs of glue. Tissue papers and magazine pages can be lightly ironed to make them crisp. Cellophane can also be ironed very gently if it is first placed between two sheets of paper – but cellophane is best abandoned if very badly crumpled as this light ironing will have little effect. It is a good idea to start by laying a few pieces of paper on the table to form the basis of your composition. Make a quick sketch on rough paper and use this as a guide for gluing into position. As you get more skilled, and your feeling for contrasting and complementary textures, colours and designs develops, you will probably find it unnecessary to make this preliminary testing and can rely on your creative judgment to build and glue your collage.

Mixed media collage pictures

Other materials besides paper can be incorporated into a collage and worked into a design to give greater depth and atmosphere, or to highlight a certain aspect of the composition.

Basically, the methods are the same as previously described. To make these collages, you will need the same materials and tools as before – plus, of course, additional materials of your choice and adhesives suitable for sticking them down firmly.

Below: Basic patterns for 'Red and Silver collage' (right).

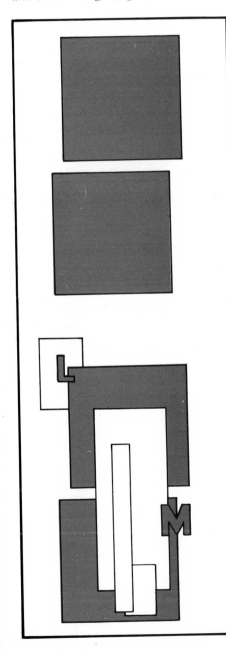

Unification by colour

An interesting collage can be made quite quickly and simply by putting together all sorts of objects and materials that are not necessarily closely related in subject matter, but are unified by a colour scheme.

The three-dimensional 'Red and Silver' collage illustrated here is a well executed example of this style.

As you can see, the materials used in the collage are very diverse. They could have resulted, all too easily, in a messy composition that would prove tiring to the eye. But, because the designer has disciplined the work, the various oddments are clearly held together to form a very pleasing composition.

The two main elements of restraint involved are careful use of colour and basic simplicity of line. Note how the background silver is picked up again and again throughout the design, first by the silver braid, then with the toy bike, metallic silver disc, necklace clasp and safety pins.

Equally the use of red is well balanced with some solid blocks of colour (shiny surfaced paper squares, bricks raided from the children's toy box, and the ballpoint pen), and other, lighter, more airy touches – the playing cards and the amusing sparkling bright teardrop shapes from a broken necklace.

Stark simplicity has been used to arrange the background shapes. Not only are the red paper shapes set firm and square, but the rest of the composition has been built up to echo their careful formality.

Note the emphasis on upright vertical lines in positioning the crossword puzzle, the transparent plastic ruler, the king of diamonds and even the plastic letters. This gives a sense of order and provides an excellent foil for small areas of movement. In fact, it is precisely because of this restrained background that the directional arrangement of safety pins and the angled elephant card gain in impetus and so successfully lead the eye to the central focal point of the composition.

Using contrasts for impact

A very effective method of emphasizing the interest of a paper collage is to incorporate other materials the textures of which contrast strongly with the paper – thus throwing each and every item into bold relief.

Left: This chesspiece knight has been composed mainly from newspaper which has been pleated, folded and scalloped to show every variety of newsprint.

Right: A 'Queen of Hearts' collage is fun to make, and colourful in effect. It involves a mixture of components.

On the other hand subtle effects are achieved by using one type of paper only, showing every aspect of that paper and then adding other materials which, although quite different in texture, echo the same qualities and tone as the paper itself.

An example of such enhancement is shown in the charming 'Chesspiece Knight' collage photographed here. Newspaper is a wonderful and inexpensive source of material. It is used in a highly decorative manner for the knight, so as to show to full advantage the many variations of newsprint – from tightly printed dark areas and bold headlines interspaced with white, through grey photographic areas, to creamy white spaces.

The paper is pleated, scalloped, fringed and double folded for added interest and the non-paper details (bits and pieces taken from sewing and jewelry boxes) make delicate finishing touches. The broken chain necklet, trouser hooks and eyes, shirt buttons, pearls and scraps of sandpaper harmonize with their background – nothing jars. Their colours reiterate the creamy grey newsprint tones, and they seem to fit quite naturally into this very ingenious composition.

If you are enthusiastic about making mixed media collages, make a collection of materials. The following list gives a rough idea of the kinds of objects you should collect. Buttons, beads, bangles, curtain rings, studs, hooks and eyes, cotton reels [spools], safety pins, shoelaces, rubber bands, paper clips and fasteners, clothes pegs [pins], glass bottles, old china plates, corks and bottle tops, mirrors, match boxes and spent matches, cigarette packs, pipe cleaners and spills, cardboard boxes and cylinders.

The only real problem is storage. However clear plastic or glass jars or boxes for the small items, and a selection of different sized plastic bags for the larger ones will help classification and identification of your collection.

'Queen of Hearts' Collage

This 'Queen of Hearts' collage has been designed by Sue Norris, and is an excellent example of how to use a variety of materials. It is mounted on a brown panel, with the design extended beyond the card onto the panel. The background is in sheets and tile-like squares of aluminium foil, with the Queen's head and neck in white felt. Features are in felt, ribbon and foil, softened with net. Gold and silver doilies have been used to suggest a lace ruffle, and velvet ribbon woven into an intricate pattern for the stylized costume. A third dimension is introduced into the collage with two artificial roses as a finishing touch.

Needlework pictures

For generations of women, needlework has not only been a mundane necessity but also an expression of their sense of design and creativity. Anyone who is fortunate enough to be able to visit museums which display the superb tapestries of the past will appreciate the sheer artistry of this medium. The great medieval tapestries are particularly distinctive for their dramatic effects, and it is a constant delight to see how alive and full of movement these stitched pictures are. Victorian samplers are another example of this kind of picture making and a modern interpretation can also be very attractive, as shown in these projects. Everyone who enjoys embroidery will be tempted to try one of the designs in the following pages. They range from a very simple but bold use of colour contrast for the landscape, to the delicate interplay of contrasting knots and stitches for the enchanting trellised garden, with its sense of timelessness and tranquillity.

Landscape in satin stitch

Pictures can just as well be made in embroidery. This country landscape is worked in satin stitch which is very simple, even for those who have never used a needle. Because of the large stitches the work grows with surprising speed. You will need to use a frame, however, or the canvas will distort. You can work it in vivid embroidery cottons, as shown here, or tapestry wools – perhaps pastel shades, or several different tones of one or two colours, to match your colour scheme.

Overleaf the full-scale drawing of the country landscape is printed – to allow you to transfer the outlines easily onto your canvas.

Materials

This embroidery is best worked on single thread canvas 16 threads per 2.5cm (1in).

Tapestry wool or embroidery cotton are recommended. but you can experi-ment with crewel wool or other knitting and crochet yarns.

If a thread is too thick for the size of canvas it will be difficult to stitch and will look lumpy. If the thread is too thin then canvas showing between the stitches spoils the effect.

Above: Detail of the stitching, actual size.

Below: Completed landscape.

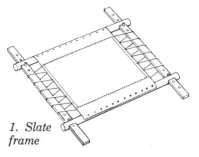

1. Slate frame

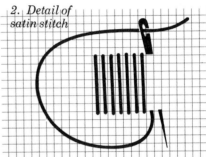

2. Detail of satin stitch

A tapestry needle has a long, polished eye that allows easy threading without fraying. Its rounded point seperates the strands of canvas very slightly to allow the yarn to pass through. The needle should be in proportion to the thickness of yarn. A tapestry needle size 18 should be used for this embroidery.

Transferring designs

The simplest method is to place the canvas directly over the design and mark the lines with a light-coloured, felt-tipped pen. If you have difficulty seeing the design through the canvas you will have to try another method, such as a transfer pencil.

You can trace the design onto tracing paper, and, using a transfer pencil, draw over the lines at the back of the tracing paper with a solid or dotted line. Position the tracing paper with transfer lines facing canvas and iron over the tracing paper.

Alternatively you can use the thread tracing method. Trace off the design on to tracing paper using a black felt-tipped pen. Place the tracing paper over the canvas, aligning the vertical lines of the desing to the vertical threads of the canvas. Tack [baste] the outlines through the tracing paper and onto the canvas. Then tear off the tracing paper.

Using a frame

An embroidery frame allows you to work with both hands and saves a lot of time, apart from preventing the canvas from distorting. You can buy a hand frame or one with legs. The principle of all frames is the same – to keep the canvas stretched taut, and it is a matter of personal preference which sort you choose. Illustrated here (fig.1) is the rectangular or slate frame which has a round bar at each end and a flat bar at each side. Webbing is nailed to the top and bottom bars and the flat side bars have a series of holes for adjusting to the length of the canvas. Webbing width varies from about 20cm (12in) to about 75cm (30in). It must be sufficiently wide to take the canvas without folding at the sides. Extra length can be rolled around the top and bottom and adjusted as required.

Framing up the canvas

Machine stitch a 2.5cm (1in) wide tape over the side egdes of the canvas. Turn in the raw edges at the top and bottom of the canvas for 1.3cm ($\frac{1}{2}$in).

Match the centre of the top turned-in edge of the canvas to the centre of the top roller of the frame. Stitching from the centre outwards, oversew [overcast] the canvas to the webbing. Repeat at the bottom edge.

Insert the side slats and secure with the split pins or wooden screws provided. The canvas should be taut.

Thread a long piece of fine string into a heavy embroidery needle. Working from the centre of the side slats and tape and the centre of the string, lace the canvas to the side slats.

When both sides are threaded, pull evenly so that the canvas threads are perfectly horizontal and vertical. Tie the string to the frame at each end. If the canvas slackens while working, untie the string and tighten from the centre outwards.

Improvised frame

If you do not want to buy an embroidery frame you can use four pices of wood nailed together on which you can stretch your canvas – attaching it with large stitches or with drawing pins [thumbtacks] or upholstery tacks. The important thing is that the canvas is tightly stretched to get a regular stitch tension.

Stitching hints

All stitches are worked in two steps on the stretched canvas. With your left hand beneath the canvas, stick your needle through the canvas from bottom to top. With your right hand above, pull the yarn through and then stick the needle through the canvas vertically from top to bottom. This may seem a rather lengthy process for a beginner but you will acquire the knack very quickly and find that this way of working is very satisfactory.

The tension of the stitches must be uniform. If the tension is too loose the surface of the finished work will look irregular. If the tension is too tight the canvas will become distorted.

It makes no difference where you begin stitching but work the whole part' of the canvas stretched in the frame before moving onto another section.

To begin stitching, make a small knot in a yarn end and put the needle in at the front of the canvas about 5-7 cm (2-3in) from the position of the first stitch. Bring the needle up from the back and work the first few stitches. Cut off the knot, thread the end into the needle and slip the yarn through the back of the worked stitches making a small back stitch to secure. For satin stitch a thread about 90cm (36in) long can conveniently be used.

To end a yarn thread, make a small back stitch on the back of the canvas and run under several stitches so that the wool is not cut off too short.

Thread the needle so that the off-standing hairs of wool are with the direction of the stitching. Run a hand lightly along the yarn. In one direction the hairs lie flatter than the other. This is the direction in which to stitch.

Straightening the design lines

If warp and weft of canvas are not absolutely perpendicular the design may be slightly out of alignment with the canvas threads. It is not important with free-style designs but, where strict horizontal and vertical lines are involved, such as in the landscape illustrated, it is better to follow the canvas thread rather than the design lines. While embroidering this particular picture, correct the design lines, if necessary, by starting to stitch in the centre of each band of colour and working outwards.

Satin stitch

This is a basic flat stitch, sometimes called long stitch when the stitch is really long. When the stitches are in a straight row they are repeated over the same number of threads (fig.2). They must be parallel and not overlap.

The length of the stitch depends upon the part of the design it has to cover. In this landscape design groups of stitches run in different directions to give interesting effects.

Mounting

A small canvas can be simply mounted on stiff cardboard; fold the canvas edges to the back and lace to the opposite edges with very large stitches. Medium size canvases can be backed by plywood 9mm ($\frac{3}{8}$in) thick – for larger canvases use 15mm ($\frac{5}{8}$in) thick plywood for strength. Modern tapestries do not require any border – the sides of the worked canvas should cover the edges of the plywood backing.

Alternatively you can mount your tapestry on a plywood panel of a larger size that has been covered with a fabric that harmonizes with the tapestry. Another idea is to frame the tapestry like a painting.

To make the landscape

Size measuring 41cm by 27cm (16$\frac{1}{4}$in) by 10$\frac{3}{4}$in).

You will need:.

Single thread canvas 16 threads per 2.5cm (1in), about 50cm by 43cm (19$\frac{1}{2}$in by 17in); tapestry needle size 18; tracing paper; two felt-tipped pens, one black, one light-coloured; suitable embroidery cotton [floss] or tapestry wool.

To embroider the design

Tightly stretch the canvas on an embroidery frame, as described above. Using satin stitch and following the general stitching techniques, embroider the landscape – following the numbered blocks of colour on the diagram.

When completed, mount the tapestry, if desired, following instructions.

Shepherd and his flock

This is an enchantingly naive embroidery of a shepherd and his flock of sheep. It is worked in cross stitch, blocked stem stitch, chain stitches, stem stitch and back stitch. The yarn in the picture is pearl cotton, used on even-weave linen. The same design lends itself very well to being interpreted in rug wool on rug canvas for a nursery. Read the previous chapter for the general principles involved.

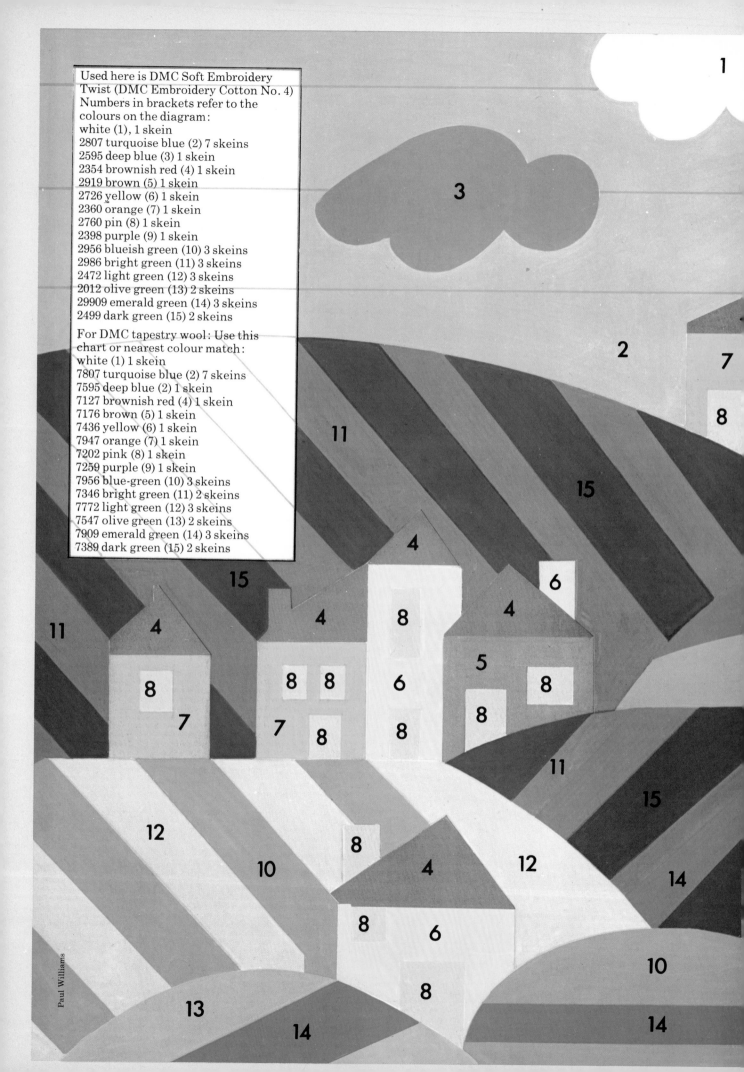

Used here is DMC Soft Embroidery
Twist (DMC Embroidery Cotton No. 4)
Numbers in brackets refer to the
colours on the diagram:
white (1), 1 skein
2807 turquoise blue (2) 7 skeins
2595 deep blue (3) 1 skein
2354 brownish red (4) 1 skein
2919 brown (5) 1 skein
2726 yellow (6) 1 skein
2360 orange (7) 1 skein
2760 pin (8) 1 skein
2398 purple (9) 1 skein
2956 blueish green (10) 3 skeins
2986 bright green (11) 3 skeins
2472 light green (12) 3 skeins
2012 olive green (13) 2 skeins
29909 emerald green (14) 3 skeins
2499 dark green (15) 2 skeins

For DMC tapestry wool: Use this
chart or nearest colour match:
white (1) 1 skein
7807 turquoise blue (2) 7 skeins
7595 deep blue (2) 1 skein
7127 brownish red (4) 1 skein
7176 brown (5) 1 skein
7436 yellow (6) 1 skein
7947 orange (7) 1 skein
7202 pink (8) 1 skein
7259 purple (9) 1 skein
7956 blue-green (10) 3 skeins
7346 bright green (11) 2 skeins
7772 light green (12) 3 skeins
7547 olive green (13) 2 skeins
7909 emerald green (14) 3 skeins
7389 dark green (15) 2 skeins

Paul Williams

Embroider a country garden

For embroidered picture making choose a theme with bold and simple shapes. Break down the composition into stitch areas, fitting an appropriate stitch to the type of texture which will best express each part. The more experienced embroiderer may attempt more detailed subjects with the texture provided by a greater variety of stitches and colours.

Background

To start with, choose a finely woven, natural-coloured fabric. When you have become more confident you can use backgrounds which will play a part in the composition of the design, with the fabric as well as the stitching becoming an integral part of the picture and so varying the texture.

Borders

If you wish to embroider a frame around a picture, choose one that is in keeping with the subject – a rose-festooned one as shown here – or a geometric border for a more modern picture. Of course, many pictures look their best when set in a plain frame.

Yarn quantities

For a small picture, such as the one shown, one skein of each colour is usually more than enough. However, if one colour predominates or if the stitches are very closely or thickly worked, two skeins may be needed.

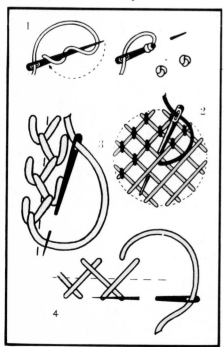

Transferring a picture design

Trace the design onto tissue paper, being careful not to tear it. Lay the tissue paper over the fabric. Using sewing or tacking cotton [basting thread] and a fine needle, sew through the tissue paper and fabric with stitches with back or small running around the outline or indicate the position of the areas to be embroidered. Tear the tissue paper away. The stitches not hidden by the embroidery are removed when the embroidery is complete.

Apple blossom picture

The apple blossom on the tree in the picture is superbly suggested by the use of French knots. These are also used on the girl's dress and hair band and this holds the picture together. Bold straight stitches which lie flat are used for the trellis in front of the bushes. These add a little perspective and contrast in texture.

The colours used are light to medium tones and give the whole picture a pretty, country air.

You will need:

Piece of fabric 38cm by 30cm (15in by 12in); one skein each of stranded cotton [embroidery floss] in each of the following colours; brown, pale pink, rose pink, light green, mid green, sage green, golden brown, white; one ball pearl cotton No. 5 in two shades of brown and pale blue; small amount of gold metallic yarn for trellis.

Working from the photograph enlarge the picture to measure 33cm by 25cm (13in by 10in).

Using pearl cotton, work as follows: the girl's dress, chain stitch and stem stitch; bark of tree and branches, stem stitch.

Using all strands of 6-stranded cotton [floss] work as follows:
apple blossom, flowers under tree, girl's hairband and part of the girl's dress, closely worked, loose French knots. Place some knots over the branches of the tree.

Opposite: Texture is created in this pretty picture by the use of different stitches.

Figs. 1-4 illustrate the methods for French knots, couched lattice, feather and herringbone stitch.

Grass and flower leaves, random straight stitches.

Background bush, feather stitch; foreground bush, herringbone stitch outlined with stem stitch.

Girl's hair and feet, stem stitch; girl s hairband, French knots; girl's arms, backstitch.

For the trellis use all strands of cotton and work a lattice, couching it with the gold metallic yarn. In front of the trellis work the flowers in French knots and leaves in detached chain stitch.

The border consists of herringbone in stranded cotton with stem stitch in pearl cotton on either side.

Work the rosettes in stem stitch from the outside toward the centre, and add one or two French knots at the centre. Work leaves in detached chain stitch.

To press the picture, lay it right side downwards on a well-padded ironing board, cover with a damp cloth and press it lightly.

Basic stitches

French knots (fig.1). Bring the thread out at the required position, hold the thread down with the left thumb and encircle it twice with the needle as in A. Still holding the thread firmly, twist the needle back to the starting point and insert it as close as possible to where the thread first emerged. Pull the thread through to the wrong side and secure if you are working a single knot or pass to the next.

Couched lattice (fig.2). Lay threads along the lines of the design and, with another thread, secure the intersections down by taking a small stitch into the fabric.

Feather stitch (fig.3) Work in a vertical line. Bring the needle through to the right of the centre line of the design and take a small vertical stitch to the right as shown, catching the thread under the point of the needle. Continue making a series of stitches to the left and right of the design line, catching the thread under the needle.

Herringbone stitch (fig.4). Work from left to right. Bring the needle through above the centre line of the design and insert it below this line to the right, taking a small stitch to the left, keeping the thread above the needle. Then insert the needle on the upper line a little to the right, taking a small stitch to the left with the thread below the needle. Continue working these two movements alternately.

Paint and needle pictures

The Chinese were probably the first people to use the impressive technique of embroidering on hand-painted fabric. The subtle combination of paint and embroidery was, to them, an ideal way of interpreting the delicate landscape that surround them. The fabric they used was fine silk, on which they applied rich inks as well as watercolour paints, and finally, splendid silk yarns, giving the flat fabric painting the added bonus of a third dimension.

To achieve an up-to-date echo of this traditional skill, you need only the most basic knowledge of sewing plus a slight sense of abandon to paint impressionistic designs on cloth. This is a technique that whispers rather than roars, and you should bear this in mind when you choose your subject matter.

Designs could be taken from sources such as spiders' webs, leaf skeletons, misty sunsets and soft seascapes.

You will need:
Picture frame, or wood, nails and glue for assembling your own frame; staple gun, set of ordinary watercolours, drawing inks or oil-based fabric paints; medium-sized paintbrush and water;

Natural-fibre fabric: this fabric should be more than double the size of your frame so it can be attached to frame; selection of sewing threads in at least two different thicknesses and in the medium-sized paintbrush and water; colours of your choice. The secret lies in harmonizing the tones.

stantial cover for the frame.

Preparing the painting surface

Stretch the chosen fabric over the frame and secure it with a staple gun (fig.1). It is important that the fabric be stretched as tightly as possible and

of cloth, to see what different effects the following techniques will produce. Read through the chapter on spatter painting on page 21 if you have not already had practice in the technique. You will find that you can achieve a fascinating variety of textures and colour tones, in endless combination.

Fabric

Best results will be obtained from using cloth that is as near 100% natural fibre as possible, since synthetics tend to resist colours. Ideal materials are: cotton sheeting, linen, calico, canvas and, if you can afford it, Jap silk.

Work on two layers of fine fabric. This allows a firmer foundation when embroidering, and also gives a sub-

the corners neatly folded under (fig.2). Work from the centre of each strut outwards to one corner and then the other to help prevent puckering.

Painting techniques

Before you attempt to start painting on the stretched fabric, it will serve as a good introduction to experiment with a paintbrush and colour on a spare piece

Opposite and above: Two really beautiful landscapes in paint and needlework. To make them, paint was sprayed on linen, then some embroidery was worked by machine, and the final details were added on with embroidery by hand. The romantic, misty effect is utterly enchanting.

These experiments will be useful in producing your final image.

Flick the end of a loaded paintbrush with your finger, spraying the colour onto the cloth in small dots.

Let lazy drops fall off the end of the brush, watch the watermark form, and think how you can employ it.

Moisten a patch of fabric first and then apply specks of concentrated colour.

Stitching

Different stitches combined with different types and widths of thread will produce delicately varied textures and designs. The stitches used in the dandelion picture include the straight stitch, star stitch and seeding which looks like very small running stitches. French knots are also used.

By building up either the image itself or the background to it by stitchery a fragile interpretive 'painting' will emerge from the combined techniques.

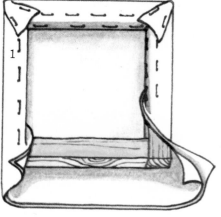

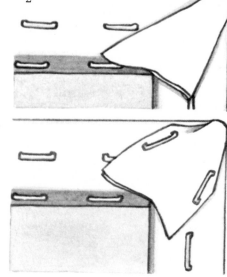

1. The fabric is stretched over the frame and secured with staples.
2. Corners are folded over as shown before stapling.

Below: A formalized landscape is created by the controlled use of paint and embroidery.

Pure gold thread couched down with silk adds richness.

Mosaic pictures

The techniques employed for making mosaics have been used for centuries, and some of the most gorgeous designs ever created have been expressed in this medium. It is a skill which requires a love of precision and a sense of delicacy, and the following projects give a basic grasp of what mosaic is all about. The materials suggested here are very simple—paper and various kinds of seeds. Most people will realize that the ancient mosaics were made in all kinds of precious materials such as marble and coloured glass —even semi-precious stones. However, once you have begun to work with seeds, you'll soon appreciate the amazing variety of colour and texture that you can create, and your finished mosaics will have their own charm and attractiveness.

À Ravenna mosaic

Mosaic is the craft of making designs and pictures by embedding innumerable small stones into a surface. It is so ancient a craft that no one really knows the meaning of the word, so modern a craft that even Picasso was happy to design for it.

The origins of mosaic go back to the very beginnings of civilization and early examples are found in many materials through the ancient world – lapis lazuli in Mesopotamia, ivory and glass in Egypt, colourful stones and pebbles in Greece. But it was the Romans, borrowing from the Greeks, who first developed the use of mosaic as decoration. Using the beautiful marble for which Italy is still famous, they made mosaic floors in their baths, fountains, homes, public buildings and squares. Even today any and all stones used in mosaic work are called *tesserae* a word of Latin origin (probably meaning four-sided).

Today, glass is the favourite material for making mosaics. In about the third century the Italian Christians discovered the wonderful colours and effects of light refraction that glass offers when cut into squares, called *smalti* and used in mural rather than floor decoration.

The early Christians discovered how to produce gold *smalti* so that artists might show the supernatural aura surrounding the Deity. Thus arrived that lustrous and magical effect produced by gold which distinguishes Christian mosaics of the fifth century onwards from all that went before.

Gradually the use of gold *smalti* spread until, in sixth-century Ravenna, it became the entire background. The play of colour and light, the mixture of semi-precious stones and glass, the sheer life that these mosaics have when seen shimmering on the walls of a darkened church is unparallelled anywhere in the world.

Traditional materials

Gold *smalti* were made in Ravenna, as they are made today, by fusing a thin layer of gold leaf between two pieces of glass, but the methods of applying them have changed. Originally a plaster of slaked lime and sand was applied to a wall and the artist, called the 'imaginary' in old documents, came and drew his previously prepared design in the wet plaster. Trained workers then laboriously put in row after row of *smalti* over the artist's outline.

Present-day building schedules do not allow for artists and their assistants to sit around on scaffolding for several years, so craftsmen must lay out the whole mosaic on sections of paper and fix them into the wall in large blocks as quickly as possible.

Beginning mosaic work

Obviously it is beyond the scope of the beginner to try to reproduce in *tesserae* any of the mosaics illustrated here, but it can be done with remarkable ease using paper. This makes a handsome decoration as well as giving a genuine sense of the mosaic technique – the pleasure of it and the problems that the craftsman must solve, such as the use of colour, shaping of squares to fit the design and, very important, the sense of correct spacing.

Copying a Ravenna mosaic

First study the detail of the ceiling from the tomb of Galla Placidia, then look at the line drawing and photograph.

Basically the design is a multi-petalled flower surrounded by six circles and two alternating leaf motifs. It is really quite simple and this is the first thing about mosaic that beginners should understand: the basic design, whatever the project, needs to be strong and simple. The quality of the finished work will come from the colour and texture.

You will need:

Paper – white, gold and five shades of blue; strong grey card [cardboard], at least 81cm (32in) square, for backing; paper, glue and applicator; scissors; saucers or jar lids to hold paper squares.

The paper you require may be difficult to obtain in the exact shades at your local art supplier but you will find something near enough. Saving old magazines is another way of collecting paper for mosaics. Many shops sell very thin and rather crudely coloured paper squares which are already gummed on the back, but with the possible exception of gummed gold, these are not really suitable for this project.

Opposite: Examples of mosaics old and new. Top, left and right: are details of the tomb of Galla Placidia in Ravenna. Below left is a mosaic designed by Picasso.

If possible, take your paper and card home flat: once they have been rolled they are difficult to straighten again satisfactorily.

To begin, make yourself a stock of 'mosaic' by cutting 12mm (½in) strips of paper and then cutting these into squares. If you can do this freehand, rather than drawing them out first, it will be better; your squares will be nearer to real *smalti* which are never exactly square. Keep each colour in a separate saucer or lid so that you can easily find the right shades when you are working.

To find the centre of the grey card [cardboard], draw diagonal lines from the corners. The centre will, of course, be the point where they cross.

Now draw lines in the shape of a cross from left to right and top to bottom as in the diagram (fig. 1). This will give you the basic linear structure of the mosaic design which is eight petals and eight gold leaves.

To find the size of each area in the design, look first at the golden centre of the 'flower'. It has three pieces of mosaic going across and each piece, already cut in paper, is 12mm (½in). Therefore the centre circle will be 36mm (1½in) in diameter. From this simple fact the other areas can be worked out with very little trouble.

The white petals are exactly double the diameter, or 7.2cm (3in), in length, so the work at this stage will be 18cm (7½in) across. Then 20.5cm (8½in) to the outer edge of the navy circle, 23cm (9½in) to the outside edge of the light blue circle, 28cm (11½in) to the outside of the double circle, 31cm (12½in) to the outside of the white circle, and so on. Before you begin to apply the paper *tesserae* you will want to pencil in a basic outline of the circles and petals. This can be done using a ruler and a compass to draw the circles, but it is best, when working with mosaic, to cultivate a freehand approach as far as possible. Your outline should be a guide not a precise statement since mosaic is not laid by precision methods and spacing will cause considerable variation in the original outline. Also your aim is to get the feel of mosaic and not to do an accurate museum copy.

To apply paper tesserae
Take nine gold squares and place them in the centre circle. The central cross will fit, but the four side pieces will need to be shaped with scissors to fit the circle (fig. 2a and 2b). When you have positioned these in the right place, take your glue brush and, one at a time, lightly glue the back of each one and press it into place. Do not

attempt to pre-glue several at a time, they just curl up and will be wasted.

When the gold circle is completed, take a clean piece of paper, put it over the area of mosaic and really rub it down; this ensures that all the edges are stuck down.

Laying the petal design
To lay the petals, note first that they are shaded, a mid-blue next to the gold, then pale blue changing to white, and not all of them are exactly alike. This is the art of mosaic which is to produce subtle variety in very simple ways. A certain primitive quality made by the irregularities is part of the charm and fun of working with mosaic.

From working out that each petal is 7.2cm (3in) it would seem you should use six rows of *tesserae*, but this is not so. You need only five, as you must allow spaces between the stones for cement. To get this effect when you are using paper, simply leave the grey of your card [cardboard] to show through to represent cement and also to accustom yourself to correct mosaic spacing.

Below: The diagrams illustrate the methods used to make the paper copy of the Ravenna mosaic.

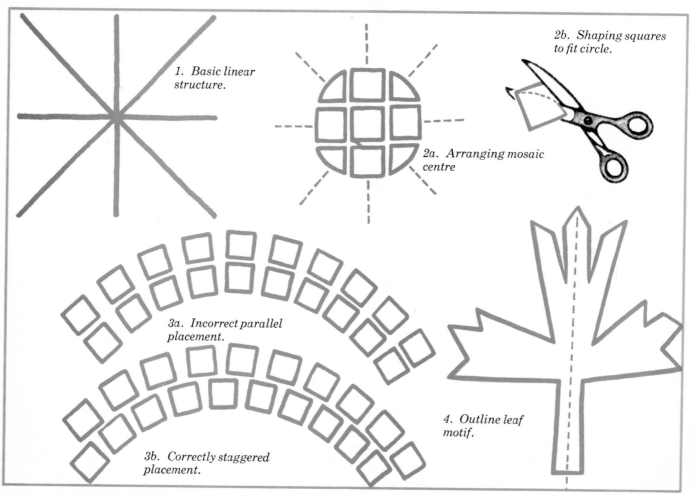

1. Basic linear structure.

2b. Shaping squares to fit circle.

2a. Arranging mosaic centre

3a. Incorrect parallel placement.

3b. Correctly staggered placement.

4. Outline leaf motif.

Left: Use this close-up of the completed mosaic as a guide to pasting down the tesserae. *A picture of the original is shown on page 51. It is a decoration on a vaulted tomb made in the sixth century.*

Use full-size squares down the middle of your petal and cut wedge-shaped ones to fill in the sides. A careful look at the reproduction will show you the best way of doing this. When you have a lot of experience you will be able to stick as you go, but to begin with arrange each petal before gluing individual squares.

When you have completed all eight petals, put a heavy weight on your card [cardboard] – large books are usually the answer – and let it dry flat.

Laying the circles

To continue, start by filling in the navy blue background as you did for the petals, pre-cutting your wedges, gluing a section at a time and pressing it down as you go.

Then tackle the pale blue circle, spacing out the squares and leaving room for cement. When you have what seems to you a good, even spacing all the way around, glue the squares into place.

Staggering the spacing is one of the constant problems in mosaic and it arises when you come to the double blue circle. If you place the squares accurately in line with each other, as in fig. 3a, you get lines running through both ways and also more cement showing because there is more space to fill in the second ring.

But if you stagger the joins, as in fig. 3b, you get more of a brickwork effect and a better visual arrangement, as you are making lines in one direction, not two.

When laying the double circle you will see that it is impossible to stagger the squares throughout since more squares are needed to complete the second circle and so, as is often the case with mosaic, you must bend the technique to meet special circumstances. In this case it is probably best to start by staggering the joins of the first circle in relation to the joins of the pale blue circle and to let the second dark blue circle look after itself, accepting the fact that occasionally the joins will be in line with those in the previous one. If you are leaving adequate cement spacing between the different colours, your second dark blue row will have taken you into the area earmarked for white, but once the circles have been established these lines won't matter.

Ultimately you have to acquire an eye for spacing which comes from practice and looking at good mosaic. This is another reason why it is worthwhile copying a Ravenna mosaic.

Next lay the single white circle and the double gold one. Notice how uneven the outer edge of the gold circle is, how it moves in and out of the navy blue, subtly suggesting that it is a rosette.

Copy this effect using gold and, subsequently, navy squares and then add the final circle of gold. You should be able to glue as you go with this last circle, having benefitted from experience.

Take a large sheet of clean paper, put it face down and rub it right over the surface, which by now will be some 46cm (18in) across, and again put the whole thing under weights to dry.

Surrounding details

You are now ready to draw the surrounding leaf motifs. The larger ones will be about 15cm (6in) from base to tip. In the original mosaic each leaf varies slightly and by drawing each one freehand around the existing lines, as in fig. 4, you can get the same effect. If you prefer, however, you can draw one freehand and, using tracing paper, copy it in the other seven places. This applies also to the little blue leaf tips which are about 7.2cm (3in) in length and placed centrally between the gold leaves. When they have been sketched in, glue the gold leaves and then the blue ones, taking care to shade the two blue colours and to add a gold edge on the tip as illustrated. Press to dry.

The background

To fill in the background in dark blue, note how the squares start by following the circle pattern and then gradually, almost imperceptibly, ease out to run in straight lines. The best way to set the background is the most important part of the mosaic craft, and the Ravenna mosaic is a beautiful example.

To finish

The finished size of your mosaic depends somewhat on spacing, the drawing of the leaves and how much of the background you wish to include, but it is unlikely to be smaller than 79cm (31in) square. If the card you are using is larger than you wish to fill, after the mosaic is completely dry, shear off the edges with a trimming knife or, if the card [cardboard] is not too thick, scissors.

You can give more sparkle and glass-like appearance to the surface by using a paper varnish. The spray type, although more expensive, is the easiest to use. The varnish will also protect the surface if you want to use your mosaic as an improvised table centre for a party or some special display.

To protect your design in a more permanent way it can be framed and can then be used as a mosaic tray.

Mosaics from grocery seeds

Grocery seeds are an ideal material for collage. If you have never considered them before, look into your store cupboard and examine the rice, beans, peas, lentils, and so on, among your staple foods. In even the most meagre collection you will see a surprising variety of form. Handle them and you will begin to appreciate their potential: the glossy jackets of haricot [kidney] and red beans, the cool translucency of pudding rice and the sequin shape of split peas and lentils, go to make seed mosaic as satisfying to the fingertips as to the eyes.

Another advantage is that, unlike other types of mosaic where the units are basically the same, with seeds you can choose the size and shape to suit your needs and mix different seeds to get the effect you want.

Grocery seeds

Naturally the seeds most readily available are those of the grocery type, in other words those which may be purchased by the kilogram or the pound from stores and supermarkets.

Most inexpensive and useful are the various kinds of rice: short fat pudding, long grain and brown rice. Being of a linear shape they are easy to handle and make fine lines for descriptive work. Rice can be polished or unpolished. Two additional advantages of the polished types of rice are their absorbency and translucency.

Perhaps the widest variety you will find will be in the pea and bean families. Whole green peas, split green or yellow peas and, less commonly, chick peas. Chick peas have an amusing knobbly shape like a little trussed chicken and their colour contrasts pleasantly with the green peas. (Beware ot relying too strongly on the colour of split green peas, however, as this is due to a dye, the original green outer skin having been removed.)

Beans offer even more scope. You will surely find white haricot [kidney], butter and soya beans which, though coloured similarly, vary in size and shape. A favourite bean is the glossy red bean which is used for chilli con carne. A packet will contain assorted sizes ranging from 1cm (⅜in) to 2.5cm (1in) and the wonderful deep crimson colour shows up excellently in a picture.

Delicatessens and specialist food shops offer a greater choice because these shops generally stock oriental and continental foods including, of course, the types of peas and beans which are peculiar to those parts of the world. The tiny green beans called moong or mung and the aptly named black-eyed beans are attractive. You may also find gunger peas which are mostly a creamy mushroom colour with russet speckles, although some are completely russet.

Lentils and barley can be found in many areas and the more comprehensive shops may have large red, green or even white blanched lentils.

Spices and nuts

Seeds of the spice variety, such as peppercorns, poppy, cardamom, dill and sesame are sold by the ounce or gram, and work out rather expensive. They are not really worth buying with the exception of poppy seeds or maw, which is a beautiful natural blue. (Maw is best bought from a birdseed merchant or raided from your parrot.)

Do not ignore nuts either: hazel, brazil, almond and, of course, walnuts. These are seeds, too, and what they may lack in colour content they more than make up for in their shape and texture.

Materials

Apart from seeds, which are of course the most important element of this craft, the only materials you will require are a baseboard, glue and varnish to finish.

The baseboard should be rigid enough to support the weight of the seeds and can be whatever shape or colour you require. Fairly stiff mounting cardboard is suitable for smaller collages but if you intend to tackle anything larger than 30cm (12in) square you would be better off with hardboard, plywood, chipboard or some such material. Many hardware or DIY shops will sell you an off-cut of one of these quite cheaply. The baseboard may be left in its original colour or it can be painted to harmonize or contrast with the seeds. If you choose to use stiff cardboard then you can purchase it in a variety of colours.

It is essential that you employ a suitable glue to stick down your seeds. Use the 'instant' type, ie those which will set within one or two minutes, and preferably choose one which will dry transparent. Copydex [Duco Cement] is a useful all-purpose and easy to spread adhesive.

Above: Seeds are usually placed with tweezers for accuracy.

Seed pictures benefit immensely from a light coating of varnish which not only heightens their glossiness but also strengthens the bonding of the seeds to the baseboard. Use a clear polyurethane gloss varnish and apply it with a brush. Varnish may also be purchased in a spray can which is less trouble though more expensive.

Tools

You will need very little in the way of tools: a pair of tweezers, a plastic cocktail stick or similar strip of plastic, several paper tissues and perhaps a craft knife for splitting any seeds which are too large and a brush for varnishing.

Tweezers are a must for seed work, both for positioning seeds and for removing badly placed ones, stray hairs, fluff or scraps of dried glue. Your fingers are just not sensitive enough.

The plastic stick or strip will be used for spreading the glue and generally poking the seeds around.

Use the tissues to keep the tweezers clean and free from glue and also to remove regularly any build up of glue.

Opposite: The key to the seeds represent: A dried green beans, B lupini, C green lentils, D haricots, E yellow split peas, F chick peas, G butter beans, H borlotti, I kalay, J red lentils, K black beans, L sugar beans, M yellow split peas, N Moong, O azuki, P blanched lentils Q Dutch brown beans, R soya beans, S black-eyed beans, T split kalay, U red kidney beans, V brown lentils.

Mosaic picture table top

Tables with tops covered in seedwork are best put under glass like the one shown, but designs can also be worked on old table tops and then covered with at least three coats of polyurethane varnish. However, for uncovered designs of this type you should try to choose seeds which are roughly the same height when laid so that the surface will be as smooth as possible. It is also possible of course to hang the mosaic as a framed picture.

The dimensions of the mosaic in the table shown are 62cm (24½in) × 45cm (18in) and the pattern given (fig. 2) could be used either in full or in part to make a similar table.

The key shows where the seeds are laid. Those used here are as follows: dried peas, butter beans, red beans, haricot [kidney] beans, mung beans, Cyprus tares, lentils, yellow split peas, Sudanese dari, paddy rice, rhubarb seeds, marrow seeds, gold of pleasure, rose hips, coffee beans. It is unlikely that any household would have most of these in stock, but something similar could be used.

Work the design following the key. If you intend to cover the table with glass you will need to split the rose hips to make an even surface.

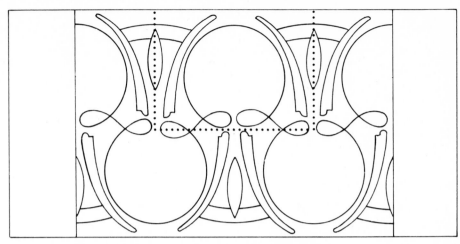

Top: Diagram of the table mosaic shown opposite. The pattern can be used in its entirety as in the photograph or a section could be used to cover a smaller table or other types or surface.

Below: This graph pattern is a section of the table mosaic design and a guide to seed placement. Since several types of seeds are used in the design shown however, its possible to substitute those given with seeds of your own choice or ones which you may find it easier to obtain. The table shown here was designed and made by Roger Marsh.

A. Dried peas
B. Butter beans
C. Red beans
D. Haricot beans
E. Mung or moong beans
F. Cyprus tares
G. Lentils
H. Yellow split peas
I. Sudanese dari
J. Paddy rice
K. Rhubarb seeds
L. Marrow seeds
M. Gold of pleasure
N. Rose hips
O. Coffee beans

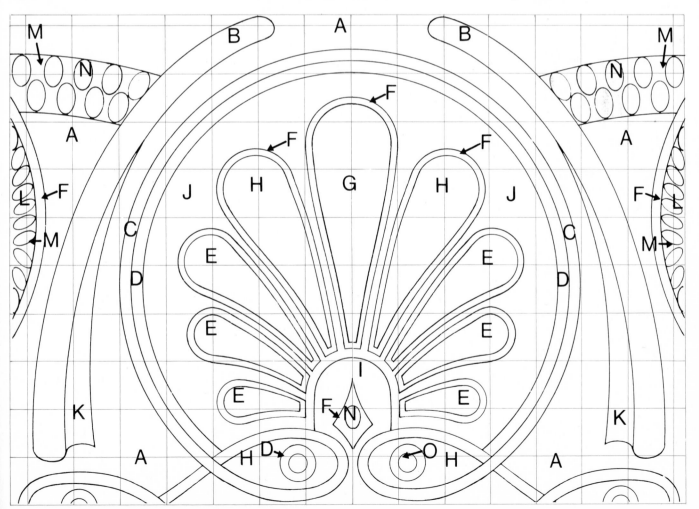

Mosaic pictures using seeds

Seeds lend themselves extremely well to making mosaic pictures and ideas can come from a number of places. One of the best sources of inspiration is from books and magazines; it is far easier to copy the basic lines of a photograph, for instance, than to get a real bird or fish to sit still while you draw it. Choose subjects with areas of solid colour to begin with and then try building textures and making delicate shading effects.

Museums and galleries also provide inspiration and both paintings and designs can be interpreted in novel ways using seeds. Dyed grains of rice, for example, could be employed to make a seed picture based on a work by Seurat – each grain representing the 'pointillism' that characterizes this artist's work.

Abstract and geometric patterns lend themselves as readily as representational ones and can serve to underline the wonderful textural qualities that can be exploited. When considering a subject always try to think about this element as well as the colours with which you will be working. The more you work with different seeds, you'll be amazed at their variety

Seed texture

Texture is perhaps less readily appreciated by beginners than colour yet it adds incredible richness to seed design. Some seeds, like peach stones, are textured in themselves but others can provide textural patterns according to the way they are laid, ie face down, on their side or overlapping as in the portrait shown. The vivid contrasts of different types mixed together emphasize their respective textures.

Colour

Seeds do not come in all colours like paints and this imposes a certain discipline in design. Before you plan your seed mosaic, it is wise to have in mind the colours which are readily available and for this reason it is a good idea to make up a seed chart.

By pasting a seed of each variety on a card, grouping them in their respective hues, you can tell at a glance the extent of your working range or spectrum. At first sight your palette will appear to be loaded with whites, blacks and browns but you will also find golds, greys and greens quite plentiful. Blue is very scarce, poppy seed [maw] being one of the few natural blues.

Colour remedies are possible, however, and one solution is learning to place seeds so that the colours affect each other. For example, white seems much whiter when surrounded by black than by a lighter colour and any bright colour will appear more brilliant when placed next to a dull one.

Another way of extending your colour range is to colour your baseboard, either by giving the whole ground a coat of emulsion paint or poster colour or by painting selected parts of your design. As seeds are never uniform in shape it is impossible, except in the case of very tiny seeds, to completely cover the baseboard. Usually a small amount of painted background will be apparent between the seeds and this will be sufficient to influence the colouring. Some seeds such as rice and split lentils are translucent and the background will show dimly through. When painting a background, however, be very selective in your choice of colour, for too bright a ground colour could kill the colour of your seeds.

Dyeing seeds

It is of course possible to paint seeds but it is far better to dye them since this does not change the surface quality. Ink, food colouring and sometimes food itself, eg coffee, can be used to dye seeds satisfactorily; but for large quantities of seed it makes sense to use a hot-water fabric dye.

Place a small amount of colouring in a saucer and test one or two seeds before going ahead to make sure the colour is right. Ink or food colour may need to be diluted with water. Use commercial dyes according to manufacturers' instructions.

Turn seeds in the colouring until they are uniformly covered. Spread them out on tissues or blotting paper to dry. Do not keep them in a huddle as they may begin to sprout.

Enlarging your seed collection

As you become adept at handling seeds and fitting them in position, you will gradually begin to want a wider variety. This is the time to branch out a little and investigate other sources of supply.

Pet shops sell birdseed mixtures by the kilogram or pound: the bulk of any birdseed mixture may be jap, panicum or pearl millet which are all quite tiny and not very exciting in themselves but excellent for working fine detail.

Colour Chart	
Colour	**Seeds**
Slate grey/black	lupin [lupine], tares, buckwheat
Jet black	niger, sunflower, black beans, Cyprus tares
Red-black	rape
Chocolate brown	dark roast coffee beans
Rich brown	tic beans, light roast coffee beans, linseed, acorns, gunga peas
Light brown	sycamore keys, lily seeds, sunflower
Crimson	kidney beans
Light red	milo
Scarlet	rose hips, rowan berries
Red-orange	gold of pleasure
Orange	split lentils
Yellow	yellow split peas, clover
Gold	oats, mazagan canary, paddy rice, panicum millet, peach, plum and cherry stones
White	melon, marrow, sunflower, black-eyed beans, haricot [kidney] beans, butter beans, pearl millet, Sudanese dari, honesty
Mushroom/fawn	gunga peas, chick peas, pearl barley, jap millet
Blue	poppy seed, maw
Green	split green peas, mung beans, green lentils
Grey-green	hemp, peas, unroasted coffee beans
Speckled	dwarf kidney, gunga peas, borlotti
Striped	sunflower, maple peas

Above: Seed colours can be varied by dyeing. Inks, commercial dye and food colouring are all suitable.

Left: The subtlety of line and shading possible with seeds is well-illustrated in this portrait. Tiny seeds like millet are used very well.

The portrait shown here, for example, is composed almost entirely of small birdseed and the natural colour variation of the millet has allowed the face to be modelled quite delicately.

In petshops you will normally also get sunflower seeds, Indian corn, maple peas, tic beans and niger seed.

Gardens and woods are the natural source of seeds and although some are difficult to collect when ripe, plants such as honesty, lupin [lupine], marigold, sunflower and nasturtium throw off a remarkable quantity of seeds which are very easy to collect. Trees yield 'conkers' (horse chestnuts), ash and sycamore keys and bushes provide broom seeds, among many others. Seed cases from trees such as beech and horse chestnut and certain flower seed pods such as poppy and lily can add surface interest to a mosaic.

Many berries, though seed cases rather than actual seeds, can be used too. These dry very well, retaining their colours and becoming pleasantly wrinkled. Rowan berries and dog-rose hips both retain their bright red hue, a colour which is rarely found naturally in seeds.

Fruits and vegetables are another ready source of seeds. Peaches, plums, cherries, apples and lychees all have seeds that can be washed and added to your collection. Melons also provide interesting seeds, as do marrows. If stored for a while unopened, the marrow seeds ripen within the fruit; they are large, white and flat and are easily separated from the flesh

Gardening shops sell seeds in small quantities but these usually prove rather expensive in any substantial amounts and most seeds supplied in packets can also be grown and preserved at home.

Preserving seeds

Flower seeds may only be used when they are fully ripe or they will shrivel or even go mouldy. Unfortunately most plants retain their seeds until they are ripened and then cast them in all directions, at which point you may as well forget about trying to collect them. Therefore collect the flower heads before they are quite ripe, tie the stalks together in bunches, tie a piece of muslin around the heads and hang them upside down in a dry, airy place. Do not use a plastic bag or the heads could become mildewed. Some of the seeds may drop into the muslin of their own accord. If not, when the plant is perfectly dry, rub the heads gently between your fingers to dislodge the seeds. As long as the seeds are thoroughly dry they can then be stored in polythene.

Fruit and vegetable seeds must be cleansed thoroughly of all sticky residue before drying. Wash them in soapy water, scrubbing them gently, if necessary to remove any fibrous matter, and then lay them on blotting paper, tissue paper or dry sand to dry.

Avoid drying in direct sunlight as this can bleach the colours and spoil them. Leave them for at least two weeks in a dry, ventilated place. Seeds may be put in a slow oven for an hour or two to speed the drying process but too much heat can ruin them.

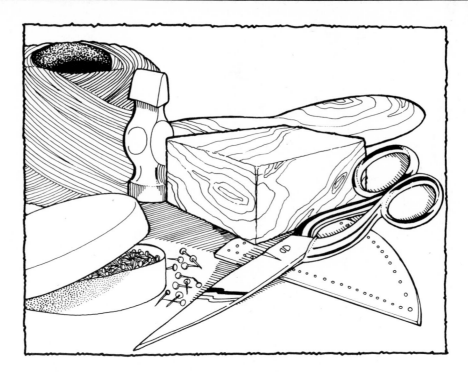

Pin and thread pictures

The art of making pictures from pins or nails and thread is immensely popular with all age groups. It is a technique which is refreshingly easy to master, while at the same time, it produces effects that are incredibly attractive. People who have never made a picture in their lives before can learn very quickly how to follow a pattern, and achieve super results. One of the main advantages of working with nails and thread is that the materials are very simple to obtain, and are not too expensive. Also, there is a surprising range of texture and colour in string, yarn and threads, especially with the new varieties of metallic threads now available. There is great variation in the qualities of different types of nails too, and we have included a special decorative panel which is entirely composed of nails—long, thin, thick, shiny, matt, silvery, blue-toned—every subtle combination that you can think of, adding up to a splendid picture for your wall.

Geometric picture patterns

The art of making pictures out of such everyday items as pins or nails and yarn has become a popular hobby among people of all ages.

The great fascination of this craft is the formation of natural curves from straight lines. By hammering rows of pins or nails into a board and winding yarn around them in sequence, curves and a three-dimensional effect develop as the different concentrations of thread create highlights and shadows. It is the angle of the lines of pins to each other that determines the curves and from this, stunning geometric designs or representational pictures can be made.

Once you have mastered one or two basic principles, you can develop your own designs. Like a kaleidoscope, there is no end to the permutations. There are many different materials and yarns you can use to vary the pictures. Felt, hessian [burlap] or cork, for example, can be used for the backing board cover. Wool, string, wire or cotton produce different effects for the threading. To start with though, the essentials are not expensive to buy – in fact you will probably have a piece of wood and some nails or panel pins [slim nails], yarn and a hammer in the house. You will also need graph paper, a pencil, rule and compass.

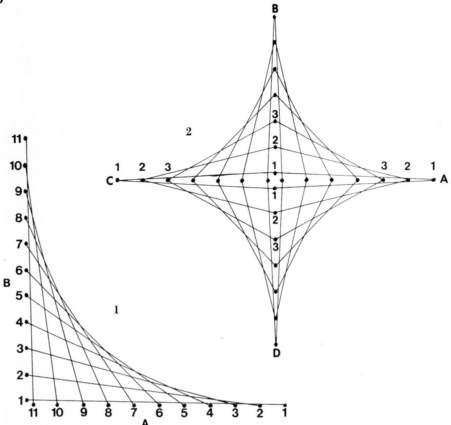

Basic designs

The formation of a curve from straight lines (fig. 1). Two lines, drawn at 90° to each other, are divided up equally into a number of points, in this case 11 in each.

By drawing a line from A1 to B1, A2 to B2, A3 to B3, etc, a curve will be formed. The closer the dots are brought together, the smoother the curve will be. Exactly the same effect can be achieved with nails and yarn, each dot representing the nail and the line representing the yarn.

One angle is taken a step further (fig. 2), with four lines at right-angles to each other forming a cross. Providing that there are the same number of dots in each line, the curve can be achieved. With the nails in position, thread this design with a single piece of yarn starting at position A1., taking the yarn around B1, to C1, and continuing in numerical order until all the pins are engaged with yarn.

A further variation on the angle (fig. 3), using four straight lines at right angles to form a square with the

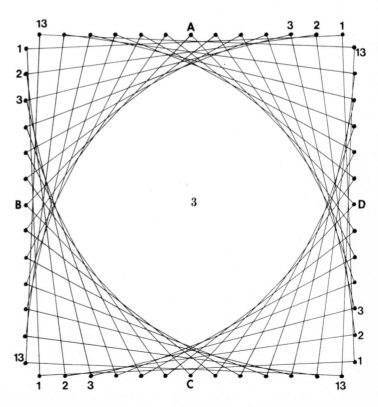

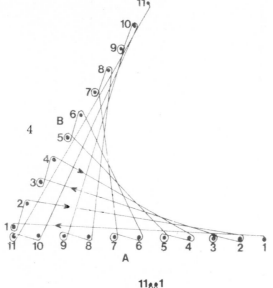

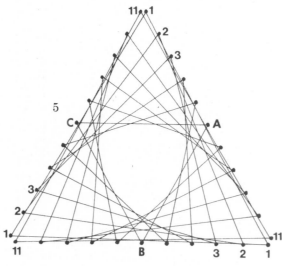

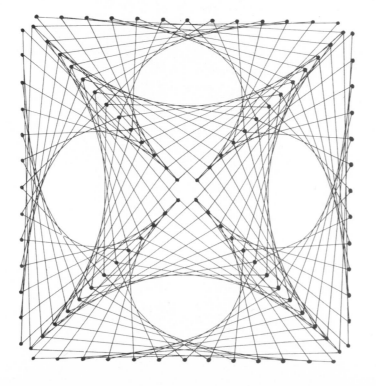

curves overlapping each other. Again it is essential to have the same number of dots in each line and to join them in numerical sequence. It is not necessary for the lines to be the same length.

To get away from lines of dots at 90° to each other, reduce the angle (fig. 4). The points are threaded in sequence as in fig. 1 but a steeper curve results.

Add another line to an angle to make a triangle and then a pattern develops (fig. 5).

From this basic triangle (fig. 6) more complicated patterns can follow. Each triangle is threaded individually but the centre lines are each engaged with yarn twice.

Making your own designs

Working from these basic shapes you can experiment on paper and make up your own designs. Draw out your patterns full size on graph paper using a dot to represent each nail or pin position. Then join up the dots with pencil lines to obtain an idea of the finished result. This will save hours of practising freehand with a hammer and nails or pins. When you are happy with the design, use the graph paper as a template and place it over the prepared board, securing it at each corner with a drawing pin [thumbtack], then hammer the nails or pins through the paper into the board.

Choosing your materials

Once you understand how the basic curves are made up with pins and yarn you will want to experiment with materials. Each sample has a different backing and yarn – the choice and variation are great. For the best effect, choose a yarn in a contrasting colour to the background, for example white yarn on a black backing can look very dramatic.

For a permanent picture the backing board, either plywood or chipboard, must be at least 12mm (½in) thick. For experimenting use cork or thick cardboard and map or dressmaking pins.

When using plywood or chipboard, use nails that are at least 18mm (¾in) long. Panel pins [slim nails] are ideal. Any nail can be used as long as the head isn't too large. The longer the nail, the thicker the yarn should be. In most cases you will be able to match yarn and nails easily.

Starting and finishing

To secure the yarn before starting the winding, tie it with a double knot to the first nail. When the winding is complete, tie the yarn to the last nail with a double knot, being careful to keep the yarn taut. Place a tiny dab of clear glue on each knot and allow to dry. This secures the knot. Trim the ends of yarn close to the knots.

Sunburst

This splendid, visually stimulating wall decoration – the more you look at it the more shapes you see – is simply made up of eight triangles.

You will need:

Square piece of plywood or chipboard 12mm (½in) thick cut to the required size; 624 panel pins [slim nails]; matt black paint; two balls of cotton in two colours.

Choose the size of design you require,

this one is 50cm (20in) square with a 2.5cm (1in) border. On a piece of paper draw the shape, using a dot to represent each nail. It is important that the nails are spaced out evenly. Number each represented nail in each triangle as given in fig. 5. Although the design consists of eight right-angled triangles, where the sides of the triangles are duplicated only draw one line. This means that the yarn is wound around the nails twice.

Place the paper on the board. Hammer the nails into position through the

Above: The completed Sunburst looks dramatic on a wall.

paper, keeping the nails the same height. Remove the paper carefully.

Paint the board and the nails. Allow the paint to dry completely.

Thread the four outer triangles first, following the numbers, and tie off. With the new colour yarn thread the remaining four triangles.

If you wish the board may be trimmed with strips of wood to give a neat finish to your picture.

Circles, moon and stars

Curves and circles are simple to do and may be used either on their own or in conjunction with the straight line designs already described to make superb pin art pictures. Also included are sections on assembling the board and finally framing the finished picture.

Covering board with fabric

The fabrics most often used are felt and hessian [burlap] but all fabrics should be treated in the same way. Cut the fabric 5cm (2in) larger all around than the board. Iron the fabric to remove any creases. Lay the fabric on a flat surface and place the board in the centre of it. Cut away the corners as shown (fig. 1). This removes the bulkiness at the corners.

Spread clear glue fairly thinly around the edges of the board that are uppermost. Lift the fabric over the sides of the wood and press it against the glued surface, pulling the fabric taut as you do so.

If the material is very thin, fold it like you would when wrapping a parcel. Glue the fabric where necessary to hold it together.

Material that frays should be spread with glue along the cutting line. Allow the glue to dry then cut along the line and glue to the board as above.

Hammering pins into board

For a really professional finish to your picture the pins should be of a uniform height. To achieve this, place the design, drawn on paper, over the board and hammer pins lightly in place (fig. 2). Then place a depth gauge – a piece of wood – next to the pin. Hammer the pin in place until the pin head is level with the piece of wood (figs. 2 and 3).

Winding the yarn

Sometimes a simple design is made more attractive by winding the yarn around the pins as if making the top part of a figure eight. Crossing the strands will also prevent the yarn from slipping off, which sometimes happens with small-headed pins.

Dividing a curve

Dividing up the curve equally isn't quite as easy as dividing up straight lines, but you don't have to be an expert in higher mathematics to achieve a good result.

The circumference of a circle can be divided up by using a protractor. Mark

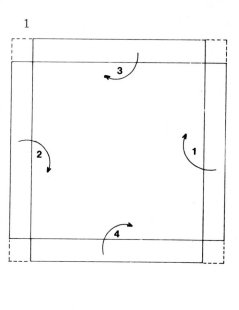

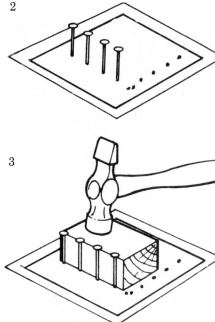

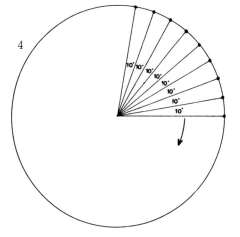

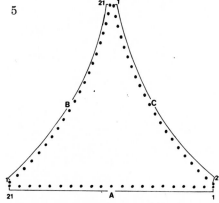

off the pin positions so that there are an equal number of degrees between each. For 36 points, for example, the pin positions are at 10° intervals, as shown (fig. 4).

Alternatively, if a set number of points are required on any section of a curve, dividers can be used. Set the dividers at a certain distance apart. To get a rough idea of how wide to set the dividers, measure the length of the curve with a tape measure and divide the total length by the number of equal spaces you wish to have along the line. This gives an approximate width for the dividers then increase or decrease the distance until you have the correct

number of points on the curve. This is a slow but accurate method.

The basic circle sample, wound in thin, shaded yarn, produces a wheel effect. The background is royal blue felt. Divide the circumference into 65 pin positions with dividers. To do this work out the circumference of the circle using this formula:

$$2 \times \frac{22}{7} \times \text{the radius.}$$

Then divide 65 into the total, this gives you the width at which the divider points should be.

Hammer a large-headed nail into the centre of the circle.

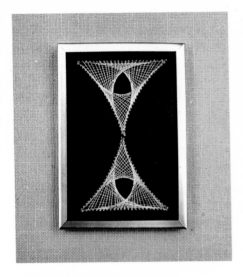

Opposite: Diagrams show how
to prepare board.
1. Cut corners from fabric,
fold edges to back of board,
and glue neatly in place.
2. Hammer pins lightly into
board, following design line.
3. Using the depth gauge.
4. Pins at 10° intervals.
5. Triangular design with
gently curved sides.

Above: Two triangles with curved sides.

Right: Variation on a triangle.

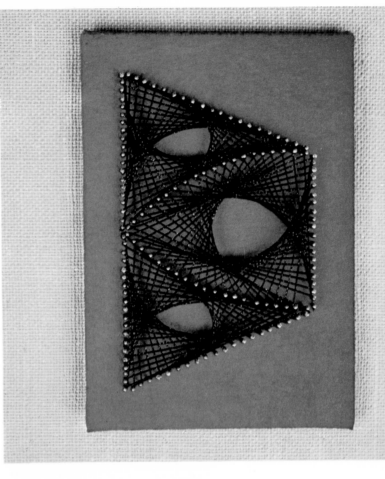

On a hessian [burlap] backing, household string gives a pleasing design with
lots of texture. The hessian [burlap] is
glued onto 12mm (½in) thick plywood.
The yarn is threaded by working around
two nails at each time. The texture and
thickness of string can be varied too.

There are many sources of yarn –
gardening equipment and fishing
tackle supply some. This simple star
shape, consisting of eight angles, is
threaded with fishing twine. The nails
are hammered into a plain board and
then nails and board are painted blue.

To thread the design tie the yarn
onto the large nail, wind the yarn
around any pin on the circumference
and bring it back to the centre. Wind
the yarn around the next nail on the
circumference, and working clockwise,
until the 65 pins are used up. The large
head of the centre nail will prevent the
yarn from slipping off.

The method of threading a circle,
divided up into 36 equally-spaced
points as shown in fig. 4, can be seen
in fig. 7. Tie the yarn to pin 1 and pass
around 13 then around 25, back to 1,
around 14, then to 26, and onto 2,
around 15, then to 27, and onto 3 and
so on, each time having 11 pins between each winding. If there are fewer
pins between, the size of the centre
hole increases, and if there are more
pins between, the centre hole becomes
smaller.

However, you must use multiples of
the total number of pins, ie for 36 pins
you could wind around every 12th, 9th
or 6th pin either three times, four
times or six times. If you tie on at 1
and pass the yarn around 10, then 19,
then 28, back to 1, around 11 then to
20, onto 29 and wind onto 2 etc, so
that there are eight pins each time
between each pin that you wind
around, this means that the centre
hole increases (see overleaf).

By threading the circles twice, perhaps using two colours, and varying the number of pins left between you can form a design of concentric circles.

Colours of a similar tone make a subtle design, for example shades of blue and mauve. On a large scale, you can build up circles in many colours, widening the centre hole each time. Wind the circle with the smallest hole first.

Semi-circles

Fig. 6 shows a semi-circle divided up into three sections: A, B, C; each row has the same number of pins. The semi-circle is threaded in a continuous sequence – A1 to B1, B1 to C1, C1 to A2, etc.

To wind the sample on the right, draw two circles and put in pins along a diameter and thread the resulting semi-circles separately in a different coloured yarn so that they share a common base. This design looks effective using maroon and pale pink yarn on black felt.

Triangular design

Fig. 5 shows a triangular shape with two curved sides. Work out the pin positions with dividers, then thread in the same way as given for the basic triangle in the previous chapter – ie A1 to B1, B1 to C1, C1 to A2, A2 to B2, B2 to C2, etc. In this case, where the curves are concave, make sure that the yarn is about half-way down the pin to prevent it jumping off the pin head. And also make sure to bring the yarn inside the curved line of the pins so that the curve is clearly outlined.

The design incorporating both straight and curved lines is threaded as three separate triangles with a black metallic yarn on a turquoise felt backing. The curved lines are common to all the triangles and are engaged with yarn twice.

The two triangular shapes with curved sides, in silvery yarn, are arranged so that one is a reflected image of the other.

Framing a pin picture

A simple frame will set off your pictures to advantage. One neat way of doing this is to wind a length of rope around the edges.

Another simple method is to nail a length of wood, 12mm (½in) thick, to the two vertical sides of the board. Remember to rub the cut ends of the wood with sandpaper to make them smooth. This method means you get an effective finish without having to mitre the corners of the frame.

For a more traditional finish use a plastic surround and mitre the corners to give a complete frame. There are numerous attractive mouldings available to give a stylish finish.

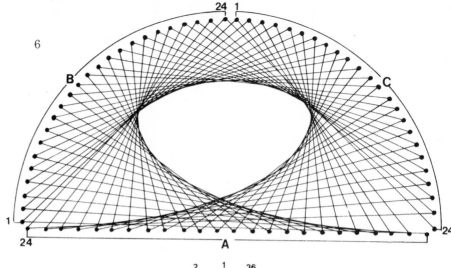

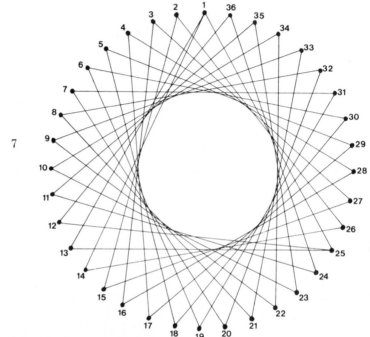

Two circles showing how the centre hole can be expanded.

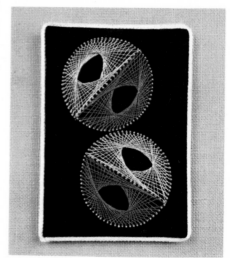

A simple design using semi-circles.

Moon and stars picture
You will need:

Hardboard 35cm by 35cm (14in by 14in);
black felt 40cm by 40cm (16in by 16in);
272 copper panel pins [slim copper
nails]; graph paper; Twilleys, Gold-
fingering [metallic fingering yarn] in
four colours.

Cover the board with the felt. Draw a
12.5cm (5in) square on the graph paper
and mark 25 nail positions along each
side. Extend the lines 9cm (3½in) to
make the shape above. Mark 17 nail

positions along each of the extended
lines. Using a compass draw a circle
which falls just inside the square and
mark off 36 nail positions. Wind the
stars as shown in the first of these
chapters, changing the colours as
shown above. Wind the circle as given
in this chapter. Glue strips of picture
frame to two sides.

Now you have completed your design,
there are various methods you can use
to frame the picture. In the illustration
shown above, a contrasting frame is
used.

Opposite above: Diagrams showing
various divisions possible
in curved line designs.
6. Semi-circle divided into
three sections.
7. The 36-pointed circle with
11 pins between each winding.

Above: The completed Moon
and stars picture looks
stunning on the wall. The
design is based on two circles
which are framed by four
bright star shapes.

Pagoda with pins and thread

This pagoda uses straight and curved lines to make a complete picture. The fir tree is effectively made up of tiny, random groups of pins threaded individually. The birds, although not wound around pins, add a light touch to the picture and suggest how other techniques can be introduced.

Pagoda picture
You will need:

Board 40cm by 55cm (16in by 22in); green felt 45cm by 40cm (18in by 16in); blue felt 45cm by 30cm (18in by 12in); clear glue; scissors; about 870 copper panel pins [slim copper nails]; 6 balls of different coloured yarn.

Enlarge the design to 40cm by 55cm (16in by 22in).

Draw the 'horizon' onto the wrong side of the blue felt, close to one 45cm (18in) edge. Place one 45cm (18in) edge of the green felt over the right side of the blue piece, so that it just overlaps the horizon and pin it in position. Turn the felt over and cut along the line drawn on the blue felt (fig. 1). This gives two identical outlines.

Dab a little glue near the edges of the horizon lines. Mark the position of the horizon on the board and place the pieces of felt on it, edge to edge. Allow glue to dry.

Finish covering the board.

Positioning the nails
Because it is confusing to show all the nails necessary to make up the tree, only the main nail, ie the one that is wound around each time, is given on the trace pattern.

Hammer groups of 5 or 6 nails, or 9 for the top of the tree, in irregular fan-shapes below the main nail, arranging them as you wish (fig. 2).

The straight lines indicate where to hammer in the nails. Most of the lines are made up of six or eight nails per 25cm (1in).

The sun is shaped around eight nails. The birds are made of two strands of yarn held together with a dab of glue and then stuck to the backing in the places indicated.

Top: Diagrams illustrate the first stage of picture.
1. Cut out horizon shape.
2. Wind yarn around nails.

Right: The completed pagoda uses geometrical shapes.

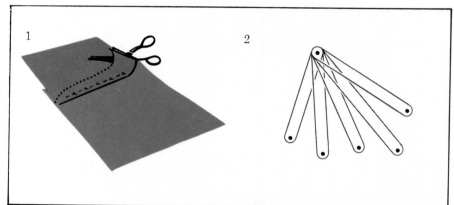

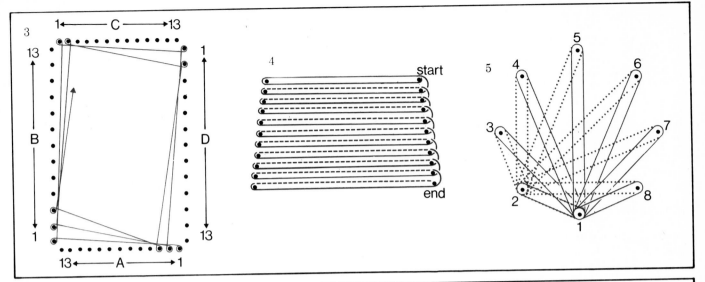

3. *Winding sequence for oblongs.*
4. *Method for winding steps.*
5. *Winding sequence for sun.*
6. *Squares on graph represent*
12.5mm (½in) each.

Breakdown of design

Working from top to bottom of the pagoda and using the basic methods already given, wind the triangle as for the basic triangle and wind the roof edging as for right angles.

Wind the two rectangles as for four right angles.

Thread the three triangles as for two triangles – and then thread the centre one, using the nails already engaged to the right and left.

Thread the three oblongs individually as shown in fig. 3. The sequence is A1 to B1, B1 to C1, C1 to D1, D1 to A2, A2 to B2, B2 to C2, etc.

Since the nails for the vertical sides of the oblongs are set slightly apart, fill the space between them with four strands of yarn wound around two nails set between the top and base of the oblongs.

To make the steps of the pagoda, wind as shown in fig. 4.

Make the fence with a pair of right angles, reversing the centre of the fence so that the angles are the other way up.

Make the tree trunk with two right angles.

Make the leaves on the tree by winding the yarn around the main pin (shown on the trace pattern) each time and around the accompanying group of nails only once.

To make the sun, thread eight times in the same pattern (fig. 5) using each nail once to carry the seven windings. Tie yarn to 1, wind from 1 to 2, 1 to 3, 1 to 4, 1 to 5, 1 to 6, 1 to 7, 1 to 8 and back. Fasten off. Tie yarn to 2, wind from 2 to 3, 2 to 4, 2 to 5, 2 to 6, 2 to 7, 2 to 8, 2 to 1 and back to 2, tie off. Tie yarn to 3, wind from 3 to 4, 3 to 5, etc.

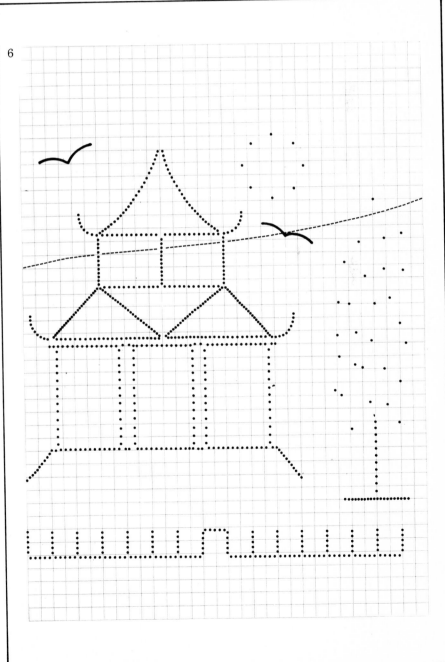

Beautiful butterflies

Picture making is surprisingly easy with pin art and it does not matter if you are not an artist in the usual sense of drawing and painting, for you can still produce some most attractive and unusual effects.

Designing your picture

The essential element for success in picture making with pins is the subject matter. It must be of a simple, clear shape which will lend itself to expression by this method – it does not matter if you have to stylize the shape as long as it will still be recognizable. Think of the shapes that children like to draw – animals are always popular, as are houses, ships, boats and cars. All these have clear shapes which can be produced easily with pin art and they do not require a lot of elaborate detail to show what the subject is.

When you have chosen your subject, sketch it roughly onto paper, modifying and simplifying the outlines if necessary to make them into shapes you know you can produce.

You may need to do several sketches and variations of your subject before you are completely satisfied.

At this stage you should think about the type of yarn and colours you wish to use. Before buying anything, check if there are any remnants left from other projects which could be incorporated into the design. A small piece of knitting, crochet or embroidery yarn might provide the different texture or colour your picture needs.

If you are making an animal you might wish to use beads or pieces of wire to form features, such as eyes or antennae. Think how you could combine colours or textures to give an impression of movement or distance. By using two tones of one colour, for example, the brighter tone will appear closer than the softer one. On a wheel you could show movement by working first around the circle with the lighter tone and then filling in between with the deeper tone.

Don't be afraid to experiment – it takes only a few minutes to undo and replace an area if it does not work as you hoped and the yarn can be reused in another way or in a future project.

Making a pattern

When you are satisfied with your sketch, draw it to the required size on graph paper. Mark in the positions for the pins with dots – the lines of the graph paper will help you position them accurately on straight lines although you will have to use a protractor to divide up curves.

It may help to use different colours for drawing the threading if the pattern is complicated with strands crossing in several directions.

Above: Detail of the gold and turquoise butterfly shown in full opposite.

Transferring the design

Prepare the foundation board by painting or by covering with drawing pins or masking tape. Hammer the nails through the paper in the required positions and then tear away the paper carefully.

Alternatively, if you wish to save the pattern, punch holes through the paper with a stiletto (or similarly sharp pointed instrument) in the required positions and remove the paper. Hammer the nails into the holes using a depth gauge to make sure they are the same height.

Gold and turquoise butterfly

A butterfly is an ideal subject for pin art because it is the kind of shape which is easy to draw and it can be worked in bright, life-like colours.

You will need:

Plywood or chipboard of required size for foundation; emulsion [water-based] paint for background, and brush; graph paper and drawing pins [thumbtacks]; nails, about 418, 15mm ($\frac{1}{2}$in) and two 5cm (2in) long; gold thread, one ball; crochet cotton, two reels turquoise; fine soft copper wire (for body and antennae); trimming or beads (for eyes).

Using graph paper, enlarge design to require size. Mark the positions for the nails and label them as shown in the diagram overleaf.

Place the graph paper onto the foundation board and secure the corners with drawing pins. Transfer the design and hammer in the 5cm (2in) nails at position B on both wings and the 15mm ($\frac{1}{2}$in) nails in the remaining positions.

Paint the foundation board and nails with the emulsion and leave to dry. Apply a second coat with a stippling movement so that no brushmarks are left. Leave to dry.

Using the turquoise thread double by working from two reels, start at position A1 and work the left wing as described in the diagram overleaf. Repeat in mirror image on the opposite wing. Complete the threading of the lower wing with gold and turquoise thread and thread the body with copper wire.

For the antennae bend the copper wire in half and twist around G1. Take each end and twist around H. Leave enough wire for the antennae to stand out from the board.

The eyes were made from dressmakers' trimming, such as daisy petals, and stuck in place. Alternatively you could use beads.

Opposite top: Flame coloured thread used over gold makes an attractive variation of the original design. Both butterflies can be made up and mounted as a contrasting pair.

Opposite below: The completed version of the pattern given in this set of instructions.

Overleaf: In order to make the butterflies shown here, you must follow the pattern given over the page which is fully marked out so you can't go wrong.

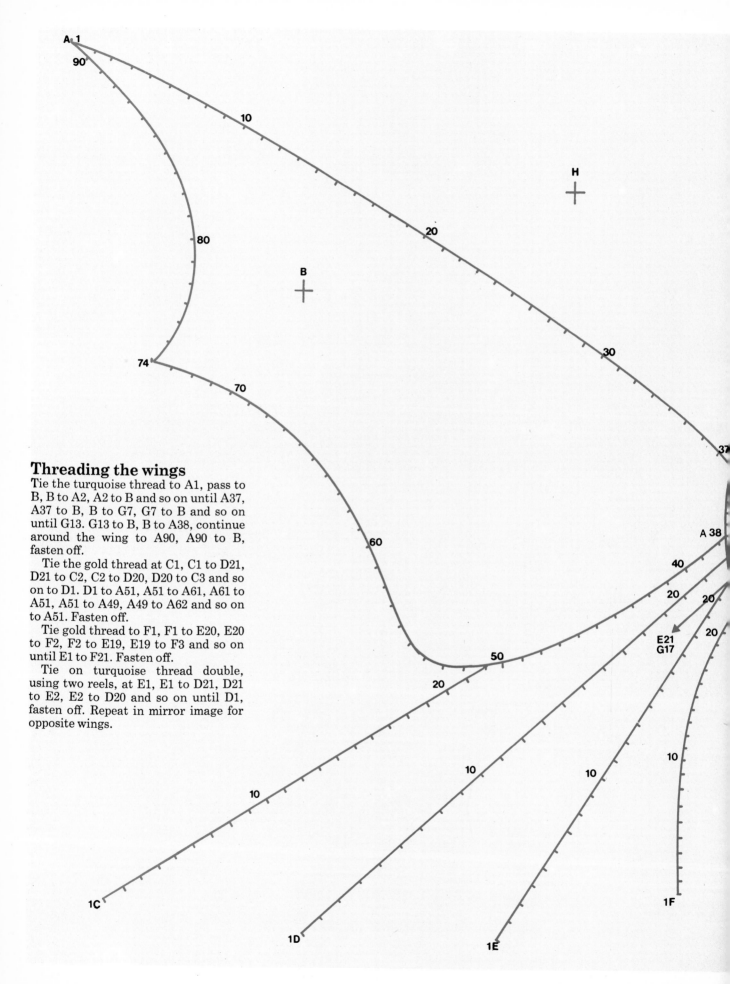

Threading the wings

Tie the turquoise thread to A1, pass to B, B to A2, A2 to B and so on until A37, A37 to B, B to G7, G7 to B and so on until G13. G13 to B, B to A38, continue around the wing to A90, A90 to B, fasten off.

Tie the gold thread at C1, C1 to D21, D21 to C2, C2 to D20, D20 to C3 and so on to D1. D1 to A51, A51 to A61, A61 to A51, A51 to A49, A49 to A62 and so on to A51. Fasten off.

Tie gold thread to F1, F1 to E20, E20 to F2, F2 to E19, E19 to F3 and so on until E1 to F21. Fasten off.

Tie on turquoise thread double, using two reels, at E1, E1 to D21, D21 to E2, E2 to D20 and so on until D1, fasten off. Repeat in mirror image for opposite wings.

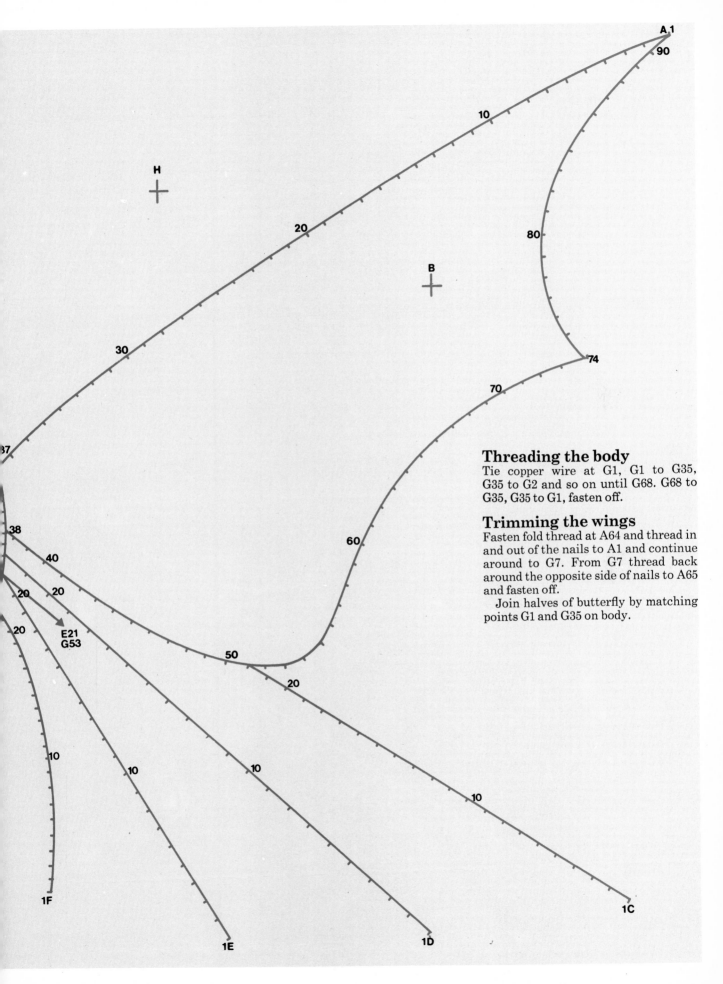

Threading the body

Tie copper wire at G1, G1 to G35, G35 to G2 and so on until G68. G68 to G35, G35 to G1, fasten off.

Trimming the wings

Fasten fold thread at A64 and thread in and out of the nails to A1 and continue around to G7. From G7 thread back around the opposite side of nails to A65 and fasten off.

Join halves of butterfly by matching points G1 and G35 on body.

Metallic designs using nails

Nails are taken for granted in most households. They tend to accumulate as more and more are purchased for various odd jobs. In themselves they are useful yet decoratively uninteresting; however, if several sizes of nails are taken and hammered into a wooden board to make a pattern they are transformed. The individual nails become part of an ornamental design consisting of ordered lines of metal dots. Whether the nails form geometric or abstract patterns is immaterial. The effect is like a drawing that is made up of a series of broken pencil strokes or spots of colour.

The process of producing these effects is so simple that you do not need to be a trained artist to achieve some spectacular results. Designs can be drawn with a pair of compasses [compass], a ruler and a pencil; or you can improvise with some crockery for the curved lines.

A working drawing

The working drawing should be prepared on a piece of stiff tracing paper the intended size of the picture. Having completed this stage the design is then transferred to the surface of the wood base. Nails of varying lengths and types are then hammered into the sections formed by the pattern. Some nails are left protruding more than others. The size of the nail heads and their colour can also be used to make the pattern more interesting.

You are not limited to a wood finish, but you should start with a plain wood surface to familiarize yourself with the materials and the technique. Once you have done this you can progress to variations. A mirrored polyester film such as Melinex [Mylar] can be glued to the wood and the design created on it, leaving some of the polyester film exposed to form part of the decoration. A thin sheet of copper can also be used to cover the wood base. Nail it in position, polish and varnish it before proceeding with a design.

The tools and materials are easily available. A selection of nails from a hardware store is probably all you will have to buy if you do not have a nail box already.

The components of a design should not be too small as they will tend to lose their shape and break up the flow of the lines unless you can fill sections with small nails.

Opposite: The completed nail panel looks magnificent with a collection of harmonizing metal 'objects' such as a set of silver keys and a delightful pair of miniature trains.

Below: A close-up detail of the nail pattern. Notice the variety of nails used, and also how the different colours and textures contribute to the overall effect.

Nail panel

The nail panel is 30.5cm (12in) square and is designed so that you can put any number of them together and retain the following lines of the design.

You will need:

Hammer; bradawl, or biro [ballpoint]; pair of household pliers – to remove any bent nails or nails that are out of line; wooden base – chipboard or plywood will do – 30.5cm (12in) square; tracing paper; carbon paper; brass dome-head upholstery nails, 25; brass cone-head upholstery nails, 30; copper nails or rivets, 30, 31mm (1¼in) long; clout head galvanized nails, 227g (8oz), 25mm (1in) long; clout head galvanized nails, 910g (2lb), 44mm (1¾in) long; wire nails with small heads, 455g (1lb), 44mm (1¾in) long; wire nails with large heads, 227g (8oz), 25mm (1in) long; wire nails with large heads, 227g (8oz), 19mm (¾in) long; blue tacks, 113g (4oz), 12mm (½in) long; blue tacks, 455g (1lb), 25mm (1in) long.

Trace the pattern of solid lines (fig. 1) four times to make up the complete design.

Place the trace pattern on the wooden base with carbon paper underneath it. Tack it in position and, using the bradawl or biro [ballpoint], draw the outline onto the base.

Start filling the sections with the nails. A brass dome-head nail is hammered into the centre of section A and then surrounded by a circle of 12mm (½in) blue tacks.

Section B is filled with 19mm (¾in) wire nails and completed with an inner circle of 25mm (1in) wire nails overlapping the other nails.

The four C sections are filled with 25mm (1in) blue tacks.

The four D sections are made up from a double row of 44mm (1¾in) galvanized nails adjacent to the C sections. Down the centre of D sections, five 31mm (1¼in) copper rivets are equally spaced to the edges. These are interspersed with groups of three 25mm (1in) galvanized nails.

The D sections are then completed with another double row of 44mm (1¾in) galvanized nails on the edges adjacent to the four E sections.

The four E sections are made up of a double row of 25mm (1in) wire nails hammered into place next to the double row on the edge of section D.

Section H is made up at all four corners of 12mm (½in) blue tacks hammered half their length into the wood.

Section F consists of a central triangle of five brass cone-head upholstery nails.

On either side of this triangle, and adjacent to sections K and the bottom edge of section C, three brass dome-head upholstery nails are hammered on either side of the triangle.

To complete sections K, J and I, hammer over the same pattern of nails found in the opposite edge of sections C, D, and E so that two panels next to each other will match. Note section G is left blank.

Coloured nail picture

This attractive nail picture is not based on a geometric design. The wooden base was given an undercoat of paint and then various colours were used

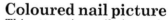

Tracing the pattern onto base.

Completed pattern on wood base.

Nails are hammered in from centre.

The circular centre completed.

Starting the surrounding area.

Nail heads left at different levels.

The curved lines near completion.

Completing the remaining sections.

The completed nail panel.

freely to create the design.

The nails were hammered in along the lines created by the colours. They vary in height and their heads are painted with the colours used on the base. This type of nail picture is very free in its style and can be adapted to more formal pictures.

Right: Colour can be added to the nail picture by painting the wooden base and the nail heads.

Below: The solid lines of the pattern form one quarter of the total design.

Frames and mounts

Once you have a finished picture, or even a whole collection, you'll want to display your work to the best advantage. Most pictures do look more complete within a matching frame, but nowadays the cost of having a picture framed is exorbitant. The answer is to make your own, and the following projects show how to achieve really excellent results in the most straightforward manner. Two kinds of frames are recommended, one sort for pictures with flat surfaces, and the other with deeper sides for work with extra surface detail such as some kinds of collage, or needlework pictures. It is also very important to know how to mount your pictures too—the right kind of background is essential. What's more, choosing the backing shape and colour is great fun, and an integral part of the creation of a finished picture.

Mounting prints and pictures

Mounting photographs, prints, pictures or any two-dimensional item serves a number of purposes, both practical and aesthetic. Putting prints between two good-quality mounting boards (one of which acts as a backing board and one of which is a 'window' framing the print) will prevent them from becoming damaged and will preserve them in good condition for many years. Even a picture or photograph of mediocre quality will be greatly improved when mounted, and small defects such as a crease or fold will become far less noticeable.

A picture which is attractive unmounted will become emphatically so when mounted; the space created around it by the mount enables it to be seen better, since it has been separated from the background and given importance. For all these reasons, it is well worth spending a small amount of money and perhaps an hour of your time to enhance a favourite picture.

There are no strict rules concerning mounting, only a number of guidelines. One of these is that it is usual to mount a picture centrally as regards width, but with a slightly bigger border at the lower edge. This balances the composition visually and is especially desirable for prints which have a caption beneath.

Proportions

When choosing proportions for picture and mount, first consider whether the picture is vertical or horizontal. Generally speaking, the mount should be of a similar shape to the image, regardless of the actual width of the border. The more you want to isolate a picture from its surroundings and make it stand out, the larger the border should be. You may decide that your picture – especially if it is a photograph – needs trimming in order to emphasize the subject matter, and this must be taken into consideration when you decide on the size of the mount.

The colour of the mount will also effect the visual size of the picture within it: a light colour will make the picture seem smaller than if it were enclosed by a dark border. These are the reasons for choosing between large and small, and light and dark borders, but all may be used out of context in order to create a striking, interesting or unusual effect. The final decision depends entirely on your personal taste.

Left: As well as simple mounts, try some other shapes for your prints. This one has been mounted with a border representing an archway.

Colour and texture

Choice of materials is also largely a matter of individual taste and depends on the picture you are mounting. The mounting card must of course be heavy enough to support the picture and prevent warping. Bear in mind that the idea of mounting is to display the picture, and therefore the border should compliment it by being in keeping with the mood depicted. A mounting board in a softer version of the predominant colour of the picture is often successful. Strong or brilliant colours should be used with care, since they may detract from the picture displayed.

If you are mounting directly onto textured board, make sure that the texture will not come through and damage the print. If you fear this may happen, first mount the print on light card and then mount this on to the textured board.

Special card known as mounting board is suitable for the majority of purposes, and can be bevelled quite easily to give a neat finishing touch.

Other materials, such as wood, aluminium or even plastic, can also be used and can have attractive results.

A simple mount

The following example is given as a guide to the method of simple window mounting which you can adapt to suit your own pictures. The diagram (fig. 1) shows a print around which it has been decided to put a 38mm (1½in) border along the top and sides and a 51mm (2in) border at the bottom.

All prints will lose 5mm (¼in) all around when they are placed beneath the mount window, so that their effective size is smaller than their actual size, do remember this.

You will need:

Mounting board of twice the size of the finished mount; picture to be mounted; rubber-based adhesive such as Copydex [Elmer's Glue All] and spatula; craft knife or scalpel; metal ruler; pencil; felt-tipped pen (optional).

Cut two identical pieces of mounting board the size of the print plus 66mm (2½in) in the width and 79mm (3in) in length. One of these becomes the backing board for the mount and the other the window.

On the back of the window piece, where pencil marks will not show, divide the board into four equal parts (fig. 2).

On the horizontal axis measure half the width of the print minus 5mm (¼in) each side of the centre and draw two vertical parallel lines (see fig. 2).

On the vertical axis measure half the

Above: Fine black border lines drawn around the mount with a felt-tipped pen give emphasis to a picture.

Below left to right: These three examples show the different effects produced by a dark, light and brightly coloured border around the same print. You must also remember to consider the colour of the wall on which it is being hung when choosing the mount.

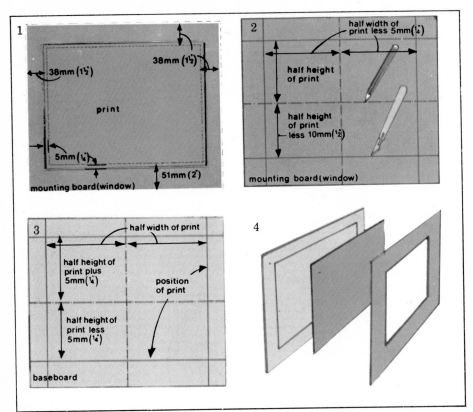

1 print

38mm (1½)
38mm (1½)
5mm (¼)
51mm (2')
mounting board(window)

2
half width of print less 5mm(¼)
half height of print
half height of print less 10mm(½)
mounting board(window)

3
half width of print
half height of print plus 5mm(¼)
position of print
half height of print less 5mm(¼)
baseboard

4

The oval has always been popular for mounting miniatures and portraits. Archways, hexagons, circles and even asymmetrical shapes can be used to advantage in many cases. Fig. 5 indicates an archway formed by a semi-circle placed on a square or rectangle, while fig. 6 shows a fairly simple method of drawing an oval by constructing two adjacent circles and then joining them with the help of a pair of compasses [compass]. You can use a template made of thin card [construction paper] if you are cutting curved lines.

Figs. 7 and 8 show a simple method of making a three-dimensional mount. Glue the print to a piece of thick card

Left: Figs 1-4 illustrate the process of measuring and assembling the mount.

Below: Drawing lines around mount with felt-tipped pen.

Bottom: Bevel cutting.

height of the print above the centre and half the height of the print minus 5mm (¼in) all around.

Carefully cut out this rectangle (see fig. 2) with a craft knife and metal ruler. (See bevel cutting, below.)

Take the second piece of board (the backing board) and find its centre by dividing the board into four equal parts (fig. 3).

Measure the outside of the print so that it can be accurately located on the backing board.

Measure half the width of the print on each side of the vertical axis and draw two parallel lines, and half the height of print plus 5mm (¼in) above horizontal axis and half the height of the print minus 5mm (¼in) below to give a rectangle the size of the whole print (see fig. 3).

Glue the print in position with Cow Gum [Elmer's Glue All], squeezing out all air bubbles and allow to dry before cleaning off any excess gum.

Glue the window board on the base board with the print sandwiched between the two, taking great care not to allow any glue to adhere to the print. (For assembly, see fig. 4.)

A fine felt-tipped pen line may be drawn around the edge of the print for decoration, if desired.

This simple method of mounting can be adapted to solve most problems posed by picture display, once the basic decisions of border, width and colour have been made. However, if you need more complicated mounts, the following variations will appeal.

Bevel cutting
Bevel cutting is a variation on the simple straight line cut with a knife. Here the blade is tilted at about a 45° angle against the inner edge of the window board (which has already been drawn) and an angled cut or edge results. This will work only on straight line cuts unless a template is made to the particular shape desired. It is advisable to practise on scraps before attempting to cut the actual mount.

Unusual shapes
Apart from straight-edged windows there are many other shapes which may be used as mounting windows.

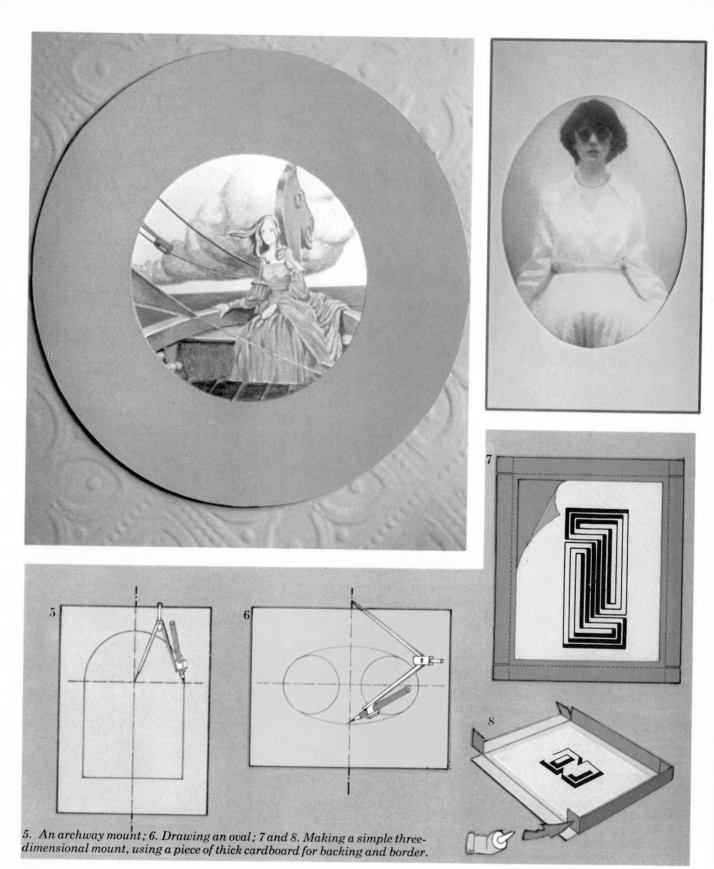

5. An archway mount; 6. Drawing an oval; 7 and 8. Making a simple three-dimensional mount, using a piece of thick cardboard for backing and border.

and measure a narrow, even border all around it (fig. 7). Then measure a further border around the first one, to the depth you wish the box to be. Cut out the card as shown and score it with a sharp knife along the dotted lines (see fig. 7). Bend back the edges and glue them together (see fig. 8).

No doubt you will be able to devise many other shapes and methods of construction to display your own prints and pictures. The important thing to remember is that, throughout every stage of mounting, care, precision and cleanliness are of the utmost importance.

Top left: An unusual and attractive circular mount reflects the nautical mood of the picture.

Top right: A simple oval mount is the classical way of presenting portraits.

Basic picture frames

Picture frames are expensive to have specially made because there is a lot of hand work involved, but they are relatively easy and quick to make. Once you have made frames for all your own prints and pictures, you'll doubtless find friends who have something they want to frame.

There are a variety of shapes available in ready-made mouldings that can be purchased from hardware stores, do-it-yourself shops etc.

There are several ways of connecting the pieces at the corner of a frame but for picture frames the mitre joint is usually used (fig. A).

The most difficult part to do is to get the opposite pieces of the frame exactly the same length. The only way to do this is to take care and learn from your mistakes. Practice sawing and measuring on short bits of moulding or ordinary wood to get the feel of it.

The mitre

The mitre is simply the term for two pieces of wood joined at right angles after they have been sawn at 45°.

There are several ways of joining the pieces but the easiest is the nail and glue technique used by most picture-framers. The step demanding the most care is the nailing itself for it is a little difficult to keep the two 45° surfaces from sliding. It helps if you first glue the pieces and let them dry in position with a string loop all around the edge, to hold the frame secure before nailing the corners.

Decide how you want the frame to look. You may have maps or prints from old books that, because of their size, need small, delicate frames with the wood painted white, black or an antique gold. Initially buy ready-made moulding which comes in a variety of shapes and finishes to suit your purposes. They are very good value.

If you intend to make several frames a mitre box is essential. It is inexpensive and is sold in hardware stores.

A

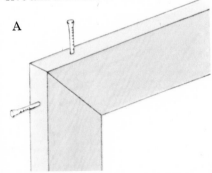

Mark the mitre box by placing the saw in each of the three slots in turn and make a slight mark in each direction on the base of the box. These will be used as guide lines in measuring. If you are using a bench hook, instead of a mitre box, carefully mark two 45° lines and cut a groove along each one as shown. Use a protractor to measure the 45° angle or use a compass and bisect a 90° angle. Saw and mark each piece as for the mitre box.

To make a picture frame
You will need:
Steel ruler; mitre box; panel saw – it must be a fine saw with 0.3m–0.4m (12–14 points); a rough saw will have a lesser number of points. A fine tenon saw will do; nylon cord – about 2m (2yd) for holding frame together while glue dries; nail punch; hammer.

Materials:
Picture frame moulding: add 10cm (4in) to each dimension of the picture and add up the four lengths. Thus for a 30cm by 40cm (12in by 16in) frame you will need 1.8m (72in) of 10mm (⅜in) half-round moulding (fig. B). The moulding can be bought from hardware stores, timber merchants and do-it-yourself shops.

Mounting board: if the picture is not going to fill the entire frame use a mounting board to surround the area between the picture and the frame.

Glass: 2mm thick (18oz). Have this cut to size by a glass merchant or hardware store. Determine the size after the frame is assembled.

Backing board: same size as the glass – any stiff cardboard will do.

Panel pins [slim nails]: fine 19mm (¾in): about 24², hooks or staples to hold the wire.

Wire: picture hanging wire, usually brass, can be bought from large department stores.

Fine grade glasspaper [sandpaper].

Wood glue.

Measure the size of the picture to get the frame size. The size of the frame is the dimensions of the inside of the rebate – ie the size of the glass and the backing cardboard. Assume the size to be 30cm by 40cm (12in by 16in).

Cut off one end of moulding as shown, with back against side of mitre box. Start sawing towards yourself with the saw tilting forwards a little. Then level the saw and with easy, unhurried strokes saw off the end as shown.

Measure and mark the piece of moulding as shown.

Match this mark with line C as shown and saw through the moulding. Repeat this to get an identical piece. It is essential that the lengths are exactly the same.

Carefully measure and saw two

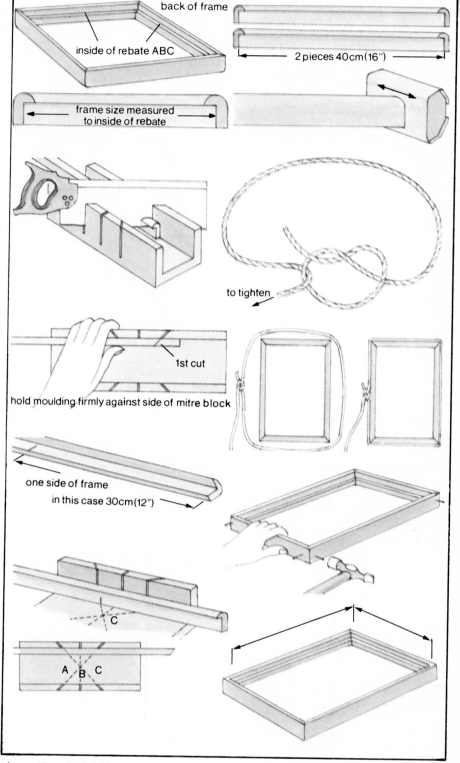

pieces 40cm (16in) long.

Sand the cut ends of the pieces lightly to remove rough edges. Use fine glasspaper [sandpaper] with a sanding block.

Prepare the nylon cord by tying a slip knot. This can then be tightened around the frame by pulling one end.

Glue the frame together. Put a dab of glue on each end and smooth it with a piece of wood. Arrange the four pieces together with cord round them.

Tighten cord, adjusting corners as

you tighten. Leave to dry.

When dry, remove the cord and nail in panel pins [slim nails] as shown. Nail carefully, holding the side receiving the nail very firmly against a flat working surface. Use a nail punch to set nails slightly below surface of wood.

Take measurements of the back of the frame and order glass to fit. Cut the backing board (and mounting board if necessary) to fit inside. Wax, stain or paint the frame.

Assembling picture frame

Mounting board is only necessary if the picture is smaller than the frame. Clean the glass, then assemble as shown. Glue the picture with rubber-based cement to the backing board or, if it is too valuable or thin, place it between the layers and hold it in position while carefully assembling the picture. If the backing is stiff and cut to the right size it will hold the picture in position once the backing board is secured.

Nail panel pins [slim nails] on the inside back of the frame to hold the layers down firmly. Leave 6mm (¼in) sticking out.

To prevent dust collecting, cover the entire back with brown paper.

Put in hooks or staples. Attach the wire securely to the hooks so that the wire will not slip loose. Do not leave the wire ends too long or they will stick out from the frame.

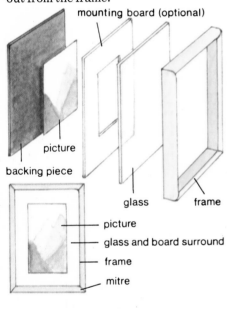

mounting board (optional)

picture

backing piece

glass

frame

picture

glass and board surround

frame

mitre

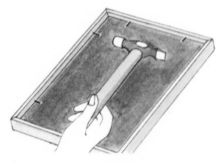

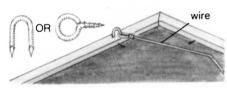

OR

wire

Right: The completed frames have an attractive and very professional appearance. Leave plain or varnish.

Building up deep frames

The advantage of doing your own framing is not only that it is cheap, but also the fact that a frame can be especially designed to suit a particular picture or object such as a tapestry. The frame, therefore, not only shows off the picture but also blends with its surrounding area.

Building up 'deep' frames to take relief pictures, such as collages or dried flower pictures, is not difficult but does need patience and a bit more work than a simple frame constructed out of four pieces of wood. The method of construction is always the same even though the completed frame may be built up of a series of frames, one inside the other.

Tools and equipment

The usual tools required for framing are a saw and mitre box, or a bench hook adapted for cutting mitre joints. If you want to make a number of frames there are two useful items which make things easier, but are not essential.

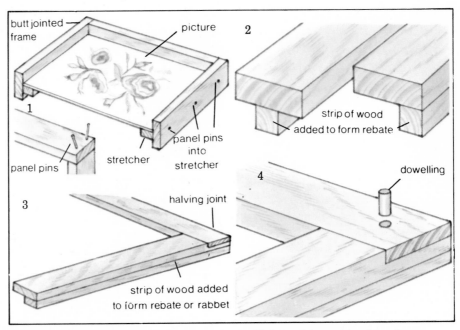

1. Frame is nailed to stretcher.
2. Diagram shows how rebate is formed by strip of wood.
3. Halving joint strengthens frame.
4. Dowelling is used to secure joint (see illustration below).

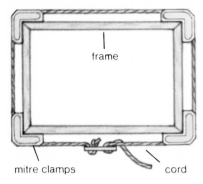

frame

mitre clamps   cord

A metal cutting block is a useful addition to a workshop. It functions as a versatile bench hook allowing you to cut mitres and other joints accurately any number of times.

Mitre snap clamps, alligator clips and corner or mitre clamps are all useful to secure a frame and to keep it in position while glue is drying.

Butt jointed frames

A butt jointed frame known as a baguette is easily made. This is a very useful way to frame a picture or tapestry which is already on a stretcher and which does not require glass.

Four strips of wood are simply put around the picture and nailed to the stretcher (fig. 1). The nails at the corners of the frame are placed at a slight angle for additional strength.

If the picture you want to frame is not on a stretcher and you want to frame it in this type of frame you will need a rebate or rabbet to hold the picture.

If you have a plane with a rabbet attachment you can use it to make the necessary rebate before assembling the frame. The easiest way to make the rebate is to glue or nail small square sections of wood or beading to the back to form the rebate (fig. 2).

This type of frame is not very strong so, for a heavy picture, with or without glass, the frame can be strengthened by using a halving joint.

A halving joint can also be used to make a frame, similar in appearance to a butt-jointed frame, but very much stronger. The frame is glued, nailed or screwed together and a strip of wood can be added to the back to form a

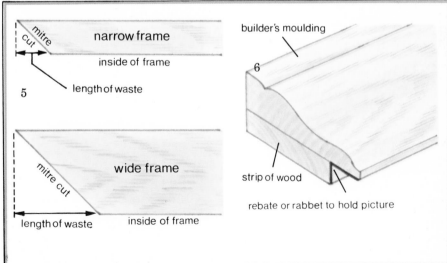

5
narrow frame
mitre cut
inside of frame
length of waste

wide frame
mitre cut
length of waste   inside of frame

builder's moulding
6
strip of wood
rebate or rabbet to hold picture

rebate to hold the picture (fig. 3).

Another method of securing the halving joint is to use dowels instead of nails or screws. The dowels are left to show on the front of the frame and can look very attractive. The frame is made to the required size, glued and assembled together.

Top left: Metal cutting block.

Top right: Mitred frame made from builder's mouldings.

5. Calculating waste.
6. Strip of wood added to moulding to form rebate.

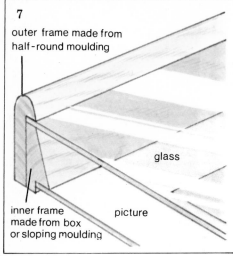

7

outer frame made from
half-round moulding

glass

picture

inner frame
made from box
or sloping moulding

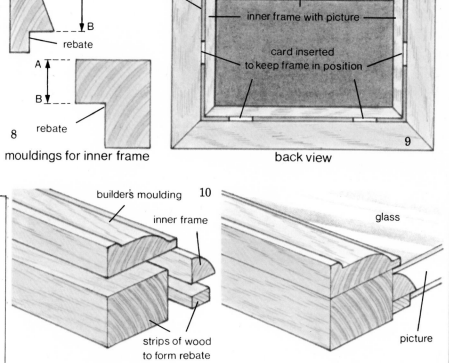

A

B

rebate

8

A

B

rebate

mouldings for inner frame

recess
between
frames

outer frame with glass

inner frame with picture

card inserted
to keep frame in position

back view

9

builder's moulding

10

inner frame

glass

strips of wood
to form rebate

picture

Using a hand drill with a 6mm ($\frac{1}{4}$in)
bit drill one or two holes at each corner
through the joint. Plus the holes with
pieces of 6mm ($\frac{1}{4}$in) dowelling (fig. 4).
Smooth the surface with fine grade
glasspaper [sandpaper] so that the
dowel ends are flush with ·the frame
surface. Polish or varnish as required.

Mitred frames

There is always a certain amount of
waste when cutting mitres so do allow
for this when measuring and buying
moulding.

The waste for each cut is equal to
the width of the moulding (fig. 5).
Eight cuts are made for a rectangular
frame so you will need an additional
length of eight times the width of the
moulding, plus another width or two
to allow for timber lost in cutting.

This is the minimum length of
moulding required. It is sensible to buy
enough for an additional side piece in
case you split or break a moulding
when cutting.

Builder's mouldings

Picture frame moulding is available
from DIY and hardware stores in
various sizes and finishes. Builder's
mouldings, however, are also suitable
and often a lot cheaper than picture
frame moulding. Builders use the
moulding to finish off doors and panels,
and for skirting boards around floors,
and cornices. (When buying moulding
make sure that it is not warped and
that it is free of knots.)

Builder's mouldings are flat at the
back so they do not have a rebate or
rabbet into which the picture, its
mount and glass fit. This is easily overcome by adding a strip of wood to the
back to form the rebate (fig. 6). If you
are experienced with a plane and have
one with a rabbet attachment it can be
used to make a rebate.

Three-dimensional frames

These are mainly used for framing collages where the glass is not to touch
the picture being framed. The frame
must be constructed in such a way that
the glass will be held firmly and leave
enough room for the picture.

Basically, a three-dimensional frame
consists of two frames – one fits inside
the other. The inside frame holds the
picture and the outer frame is used for
the glass (fig. 7). When designing a
frame like this it is important that you
know how far the glass must be from
the picture and to use a moulding for
the inner frame that will allow for this.

The distance available is indicated
between points A and B (fig. 8) on the
inner frame moulding.

The inside or smaller frame is constructed with mitre joints to fit around
the picture.

The frame to hold the glass is made
3mm ($\frac{1}{8}$in) larger to fit around the
smaller frame.

Assemble the frame by placing the
glass in the larger frame and the
picture in the smaller frame.

Centre the smaller frame in the other
frame on top of the glass and insert bits
of card to keep it in position. Use glue
if necessary (fig. 9).

Complex frames

The moulding you want to use might
not give you the necessary distance to
lift the glass from the picture or you
might want to use builder's moulding
which has no rebate. These problems
are easily overcome (fig. 10). Always

*Figs. 7-10 show the steps in
making three-dimensional frames.*

remember that each frame is built up
individually starting with the inner
frame and the measurements for the
glass are taken once construction is
complete but before the final assembly
is done.

Make the inner frame using the
builder's moulding.

Add a strip of wood to the back to
form the necessary rebate. A mitre
joint can be used but a butt joint is
easier. As the strips cannot be seen it
does not matter if the joints are not
very accurate. Use wood glue to secure
strips to back of moulding.

Make the outer frame in the same
way but use a few panel pins [slim
nails] to secure the moulding to the
strips. This will ensure the necessary
strength to support the completed
frame. This outer frame is constructed
slightly larger – 3mm ($\frac{1}{8}$in) all around –
to fit around the inner frame. Once the
two frames are complete the glass is
cut to fit rebate of outer frame.

The frame is assembled in the same
way as the previous three-dimensional
frame.

Add picture hooks and wire and the
frame is complete.

Once you have got the idea of building up frames and you have actually
made one, it is easy to continue and
design frames using a wide combination of mouldings.